Victoria (Stn)
Wed 28 Sept 1999

The Privatisation of British Rail

Crystal Palace

The Privatisation of British Rail

Nigel G. Harris and Ernest Godward

*New station signs at Gipsy Hill,
Connex SouthCentral [N.G.Harris]*

The Railway Consultancy Press

Published by the Railway Consultancy Press

Distributed by A & N Harris
43a Palace Square
Crystal Palace
London
SE19 2LT
United Kingdom

Copyright © 1997, Nigel G. Harris and Ernest Godward

All rights reserved. No part of this publication may be reproduced, stored in a retrieval system, or transmitted in any form or by any means, electronic, mechanical, photocopying, recording or otherwise, without prior permission in writing from A & N Harris in writing.

British Library Cataloguing in Publication Data:
THE PRIVATISATION OF BRITISH RAIL
1   British Rail
2   Railway Privatisation
3   Railway Economics
I   Harris, N.G.
II Godward, E.W.
Dewey ref. point 385.1

Designed and Produced by Axxent Ltd
The Old Council Offices, The Green, Datchet
Berkshire, SL3 9EH
Cover Design by Amanda Askwith

Cover pictures:
after privatisation: HST in 'Virgin' livery *[Milepost 92½]*
before privatisation: Class 47 on an InterCity liveried CrossCountry train at Oxford *[E W Godward]*
before privatisation: Class 56 on an oil train at Durham *[N G Harris]*

ISBN 0 9529997 0 6

Foreword

For the last four years, the task of making privatisation work has dominated the lives of all those in the railway industry. A slow start meant that the bulk of the process was concentrated within the 30 months or so leading up to the 1997 general election. With around 80 companies to be sold, and franchises to be let, the resulting hectic pace meant that for most of us there was barely time to note what was happening; considered analysis was out of the question.

Now, with the ink on the final sales documents barely dry, Nigel Harris and Ernest Godward have brought the privatisation of British Rail into focus. In this book, they describe not just the history of rail privatisation, the emerging policy and its implementation, but also look at the implications for transport in Britain, and consider how the railways might have been taken forward differently. For this alone, and its wealth of statistical information, the book will provide an invaluable source of future reference.

But, more than that, it provides a check-list by which the success or failure of the Government's on-going great experiment can be judged. And its financial analyses provide a form guide to likely winners and losers.

While essential reading, I see this book as essentially an interim report and await with eager anticipation the expanded second edition, looking back from 2001. Let us hope that the success of this first edition encourages the authors to take the task forward.

Roger Ford
February 1997

Contents

	page
1 Introduction	9
2 Historical Perspective:	11
Theoretical Background	12
Private Railways	13
Nationalised Railways	14
Creation of the Ministry of Transport	15
1921 Railways Act	15
1933 Nationalisation – Success of LPTB?	18
Investment in Railways and the 1935/40 New Works Programme	18
Competition and Co-ordination	20
The Second World War	22
Aftermath	23
Railway Nationalisation	24
3 British Rail 1973-1983	26
New Government and a New Approach	26
Electrification	27
Problem Lines	29
Prestige Projects	30
The Nettle of Productivity	33
The Serpell Report	35
4 British Rail 1984-1994	38
The Economic Boom 1984-1989	38
Sector Management	40
Fares Policy	41
InterCity into Profit	42
The NSE Dream	44
Sprinterisation and Regional Reopenings	44
Airport Links	50
Efficiency	51
Recession 1989-1994	52
Sale of Subsidiaries	54
OfQ and Preparation for Privatisation	54
Total Route Modernisation	55
Investment	55
Private Sector Involvement	57
5 The Process of Privatisation	60
Proposals for Change	61

	Why Privatise at All?	63
	Swedish Experience and EC Directives	64
	Parliamentary Progress	66
	Progress in Restructuring	67
	Vesting and PSRs	73
	Franchising Progress	75
	Sales of Other Companies	80
	Analysis with hindsight	81
6	The New Structure	82
	The Old Structure	82
	The New Structure	82
	Railtrack	84
	The Train Operating Companies	95
	Other Companies	102
	The Rail Regulators	104
	Impacts on Financial Arrangements	107
	Impacts on Safety	111
7	Impacts of the New System: Has it Worked?	112
	Political Impacts	113
	Impacts on Customer Satisfaction	113
	Franchise Efficiency	116
	Analysis of Franchise Bids	118
	Franchise Turnround	119
	Overall Fiscal Efficiency – Initial Impacts	129
	Overall Fiscal Efficiency – Ongoing Impacts	134
	Impacts on Companies in the Industry	140
	Other Economic Impacts	141
8	The Future of Britain's Railways	146
	Operations	146
	Industry Structure	147
	Planning	148
	Rolling Stock Replacement	150
	Electrification	150
	Signalling	151
	The Construction of New Stations	151
	The Construction of New Lines	152
	Major Service Changes	152
9	Conclusions	154
References		156
Appendix A.		
	Sales and Disposals of BR Subsidiary Businesses	160

Acknowledgements

A considerable number of friends and colleagues have given encouragement and assistance during the production of this book. Many professional colleagues have provided stimulating discussion, and helped clarify the arguments. In particular, we should like to thank Martin Callaghan, for assistance in the difficult area of assessing the franchises financially. Proof-reading by Roger Ford and others has also improved the flow and content of the text. However, as we have attempted to be as independent and objective as possible, access to internal British Rail papers and personnel has been outside the scope of this project. It has therefore been difficult to identify fully the response of BR and its constituent elements to the process of privatisation. In addition, some figures have necessarily been rounded or estimated. Any remaining errors are therefore our responsibility.

In terms of the production of this book, we would like to thank both the private financial sponsors, and John Cox of Axxent, who was responsible for the physical appearance of the book. We should also like to thank our wives, Alison and Patricia, and our children, for supporting us whilst we analysed and subsequently wrote up this interesting subject.

Nigel G Harris,	Ernest W Godward,
London SE19.	Hatfield Peverel, Essex.

About the authors:

Dr Nigel G Harris is Managing Director of The Railway Consultancy Ltd. He is amongst Britain's leading railway planners, with a reputation based particularly on technical advances in network modelling and fares policy research. However, he also has expertise in operational simulation, Stated Preference market research, scheme appraisal and railway business planning, which gives him one of the best understandings in Britain of railway business performance. He co-authored the key text "Planning Passenger Railways", which is the market leader in the field, and has published over 40 other papers. He is a contributor to "Modern Railways", is a visiting lecturer at the Universities of Newcastle and Sheffield, and has spoken to a wide variety of groups including railway staff, and international conferences in Europe and North America.

Ernest Godward has a considerable range of experience in the railway planning field, and is currently undertaking research in Railway Cost: Benefit Analysis. He was previously Business Planning Manager for the Channel Tunnel Rail Link at Union Railways, which included a secondment to the European Centre for Infrastructure Studies in Rotterdam. Before that he was involved in capital appraisal and station planning issues at London Underground. He also has expertise in market research, and in transport planning in both local government and the consultancy sector. He has lectured at the universities of Sheffield and North London, and has a number of papers to his name.

1 Introduction

Railways in Britain were developed in the private sector, were nationalised in 1948 and have recently been privatised again. Politics has therefore been important in the development of the railways, and changes often made for political reasons. The 1993 Railways Act, enabling the current privatisation, was overtly political, and was justified on such grounds. But what have its real effects been on the industry? Has it been good for passengers and freight customers?

This book attempts to make an objective assessment of the recent privatisation of British Rail. It provides a logical framework for the indicative numerical analysis presented in chapter 7, an analysis which was eminently lacking during the privatisation process itself. That process was driven by a number of motives, some economic and some political. However, some of these reasons were questionable, and we consider their validity. For instance, was British Rail really a monopoly? And was it actually poorly run? John Welsby, the last Chairman of British Rail, noted in the 1995-6 Annual Report and Accounts that "It is tempting for many to see the mere fact of privatisation as somehow a condemnation of what British Rail had been." We recognise the real efficiency gains made by BR before privatisation, and have ensured that we have compared current improvements with what was already being achieved.

Our earlier chapters necessarily give some attention to the historical context of structure and ownership because, in organisational terms, there is little new – it has largely been done before. Explanation is also given of the different possible manners of privatisation which emerged during debate in the late 1980s, since much controversy has been over the *manner* of privatisation, as much as whether it should have been done at all. The new railway structure is detailed in chapter 6.

The real core of this volume, however, is the examination of the impacts of the new system, including the impacts of the transition to it. Objective criteria have been selected for measuring success, and then evidence examined against these criteria. With all the passenger rail franchises now let, and some having operated for over one year, it is possible to make an initial judgement as to the success of the process (or otherwise). Similarly, on the freight side, new owners English, Welsh and Scottish Railways have now set out their stall, and indicated the direction in which they wish to take the freight business.

Having appraised the current situation, chapter 8 examines the likely direction of the industry in the immediate future. In the conclusions, we pull together the varying messages from the railway, and look at how the railways in Britain may build on their new-found structure over the next generation. We hope that this book stimulates debate, and enables the railway to move forward, rather than backwards, with a better understanding of how it has changed recently. For environmental and other reasons, progress is certainly needed on Britain's railways. We look forward to that too.

2 Historical Perspective:
There is Nothing New in Railways!

Introduction

The break-up of the British Railways monolith into 25 passenger franchises has begun a process which, on some routes, will see direct competition the like of which has not been seen since the 19th Century. A degree of price competition has already emerged on a number of routes (e.g. London to Gatwick Airport). We can expect to see more of this where there are a number of operators/franchisees sharing a route.

As the franchises develop, other types of competition will emerge, perhaps on service frequency or even reliability, such as between London and Birmingham. Here the Chiltern Line train operator (M40 Trains) has started to compete for traffic on both reliability and price with the West Coast Main Line route via Rugby. Perhaps we will see the emergence of the competition between the East and West Coast route, particularly when the latter has been modernised. There may not be the "races to the north", but both franchises serve Scotland's two major cities, and can compete for some traffic.

History can provide some pointers to the likely outcomes of competition. The past has a great deal to teach us, and the future success of the railway depends on taking on board some of those lessons. This chapter casts a backward look over Britain's railway history, and highlights previous examples of many of the current issues – there is little or nothing new in the history of railways that has not been seen previously. Ownership of, and investment in, the railways have been key recurring issues, as they remain today.

Perhaps the only new thing compared with the past is the degree of competition that rail will face from other modes. One of the lessons that managers in the new railway must learn is that, whilst there may be degrees of competition with other railways at the margin, the real competition that faces rail operators is principally with road transport. On some routes air and coach competition may also be important. An understanding of the theory of generalised costs used in understanding and analysing transport (see, for instance, Harris (1992a)) shows that generalised costs will be minimised where the operator provides convenience of service and minimises the number of interchanges. Clearly the ultimate for passenger traffic is often the private car.

Theoretical Background

There are a number of market conditions recognised by economists. All have occurred in Britain's railway industry at different times, and all are relevant to current changes in industry structure.

Perfect Competition

The two extremes usually considered in economics are the monopoly industry and the perfectly-competitive industry. Under perfect competition, the actions of individual firms and the consumers of their goods or services have no effect on price. The characteristic of such markets is that many sellers market to many buyers, and the demand curve facing the industry is horizontal. In railway terms, the development of many competing lines in the Victorian era veered towards perfect competition; it also led to a reduction in profits and shareholders' dividends.

Oligopolies

With industries in conditions of monopoly or perfect competition, firms have no need to be concerned about the impact of their actions on other firms. However, if there are only a few companies, each firm does have to consider the effects of its actions, since other firms in the industry may react to those actions. These are oligopolistic conditions, characterised by a small number of firms, and by some barriers to entry into the industry. These were the conditions applicable during part of the early 20th century, when there were the "Big Four" railway companies (LMS, LNER etc.). From the 1930s, competition was regulated, and the Government effectively sanctioned cartel operation. Prices and rates were agreed between the companies, and revenues were pooled and split according to a defined formula related to operations. Choice then came down only to service quality as perceived by the passenger or freight customer on the small number of competitive services.

Monopolies

Prior to the amalgamation of the railways under the 1921 Act there was a degree of monopolistic competition. Each company had a degree of geographical monopoly. The decisions of individual companies had little effect on other companies, although the industry was regulated in terms of the maximum charges they could impose (as is the case now).

Genuine monopolies are, however, the sole suppliers of services. British Rail was, until 1994, effectively the monopoly supplier of rail services in Britain, but it could not be considered to be a monopoly in the transport sense, because of an overall mode share of only 6%. However, prior to the 1930s, because other modes were poorly-developed, railways could be considered as monopoly suppliers of transport. There were certainly monopoly supply situations in the post-War period; between 1948 and 1962 British Railways were part of the British Transport Commission, which until 1952 was a true monopoly supplier of all non-car transport, whether for passengers or freight.

Private Railways

When railways were being constructed, railways both owned the infrastructure and operated the trains that ran on it. It also meant that railways developed into local monopolies. This led to regulation, in terms of the charges that could be levied on passengers and traders. For instance, the running of "Parliamentary" trains was required, trains in which passengers were carried in third class at one old penny per mile (0.41p/mile). The obligation ended in 1883, to be replaced by a general obligation to provide workmen's tickets at reduced rates. This was to enable workers to move from congested districts to areas of lower population density but further from work. It gave an impetus to suburban development around many large towns and cities.

In many instances the regulation led to the development of uneconomic competing lines. These kept traffic on the trains of a single operator but perhaps at the expense of a longer distance travelled. In addition, lines in the UK had a high capital cost compared to other countries. Thomson and Hunter (1973) quote an average cost per route mile of railway of £54,000 compared with £21,000 in Prussia and less than £13,000 in the United States. Railways therefore had a high capital burden to carry.

Nationalised Railways

The idea that railways should be controlled or owned by the state is not an idea which emerged after the Second World War as many think. The first calls for nationalisation of the railways came in the 19th Century. The Railways Act of 1844 had a clause allowing the Government to purchase newly formed railway companies after 21 years. However, the governments of the period never exercised such options. Support for nationalisation principally came from the railway trade unions, but also from small traders reliant on the railways for the transport of their goods and manufactures were also vocal on this subject. In 1895 the Railway Nationalisation League was formed, and in 1908 the Railway Nationalisation Society, both promoting the cause of a nationalised system.

In 1914, there was cross-party support for nationalisation – even Winston Churchill promoted the idea. The railways were struggling in a strongly-competitive but low-profit industry, despite having some of the highest freight rates in Europe. Aldcroft (1968) notes that the rates were determined "...by reference to a value classification of commodities, regard being had to what the traffic would bear, and the forces of competition". Early textbooks on railway economics usually devote at least a chapter to this topic of classification. The principle was that high-value goods were able to bear high charges and there would, implicitly, be a cross-subsidisation of lower-value goods. This is less acceptable thinking now.

The first state control of the railways came in the First World War. Wartime control showed how inefficient the disparate companies had become, and made action on reorganisation unavoidable. By the end of the War, a consensus had emerged regarding the reorganisation of the transport industry, and the setting-up of the Ministry of Transport. Nationalisation lost favour, however, and the railways remained in private hands, in four major groupings, under the Railways Act 1921.

Creation of the Ministry of Transport

The railways were placed under Government control as soon as the First World War broke out. However, control was not the same as ownership. The railways remained in the hands of private investors, with operation and management put into the hands of a committee of railway managers. Gwilliam and Mackie (1975) note that with increases in wages and costs, the railways ended the war with alarming current deficits.

> "Unified operation of the railways during the war had yielded great technical benefits yet they were financially in a far worse position than ever, The state, which had used the railways to such good purpose during war, could hardly escape the responsibility to see them return to a sound financial footing. With such complex problems to be faced in the transport field in the post war period, a separate Ministry of Transport was set up for the first time in 1919."

The key tasks of the new Ministry included developing an effective national road system, raising revenue from taxation on petrol, putting the railways' finances into order, and compensating them for the deterioration that had occurred during the War. Wider economic problems (including a three-month coal miners' strike in 1921) caused the deficit to rise to £60m and this effectively forced re-organisation of the railways under the Railways Act 1921.

1921 Railways Act

This amalgamated 120 separate and disparate railway companies into four major groups. Thomson and Hunter (1973) argued that, had this been done 50 years earlier, many of the problems of duplication and excess capacity might have been avoided. Ostensibly the Act created four areal monopolies. It was noted that "the effect of the new statutory grouping is to leave the bulk of the territory of Great Britain non-competitive, but the bulk of the traffic competitive". (Acworth, 1924)

The Act did nothing to address the problems of "joint" companies and "penetrating lines". The former was resolved on nationalisation, but the latter not until the late 1950s; a classic example of the latter is the London, Tilbury & Southend Line, which had been taken over by the Midland in 1906, and which became a penetrating line of the LMS in LNER territory. Conversely, the Great Central became a penetrating line of the LNER into LMS territory.

Direct competition existed from Southend – but only in terms of the services provided. Competition was not on rates and fares. Indeed, by the 1930s, the abolition of such direct competition had been sanctioned by the Ministry of Transport through the creation of pooling agreements. The Great Central had failed financially, but under LNER auspices it became a focus for anti-LMS competition to Leicester, Nottingham, Sheffield and Manchester. Only after nationalisation and cut-backs in freight did the raison d'etre of the line disappear; it was closed after the Beeching re-organisation in 1966.

The amalgamation was not without its problems. For instance, the LMS was riven by rivalries between the old Midland and LNWR companies, rivalries which were not finally solved until the 1930s. Rivalry was based upon operational practices, locomotives types, and approaches to standardisation. Clearly, this may be a problem faced in the future where amalgamation occurs. It has certainly been seen recently in the bus industry; one management becomes dominant, and the problem is reduced to a personal issue. In takeovers (and franchises), incoming senior management may replace incumbent staff.

The problems of the LNER were not those of inter-company rivalry but those of money. The group had been established with a decentralised approach keeping the good practices of its constituent companies, and dividing the company into three divisions. Many of the industries served by the group were those most affected by the economic circumstances of the time (e.g. coal, iron and steel, shipbuilding). Throughout much of the period these industries were in recession, and they suffered badly during the depression of 1930-3. However, the company invested strategically (e.g. the first marshalling yard at Whitemoor), and introduced fast long-distance freight and passenger services, which stimulated traffic.

In contrast, the Southern was little affected by the economic climate, and it advanced technically throughout the period in the face of competition from other modes. Suburban electrification schemes begun by its constituents were developed, and expanded after clear evidence of the large benefits which other commentators of the time (e.g. consultants and Government Commissions) had reported as modest.

The GWR was perhaps the group least affected by the Grouping, in that it was a major company anyway; it expanded by takeover of very much smaller companies. These included the Taff Vale, Rhymney and Cardiff Railways, which had been relatively prosperous coal-carrying lines before the war. Bonavia (1980) noted of the Great Western: "If a nation that has no history is happy, the railway that suffers no re-organisation is equally happy".

The wider economic picture within which the railway worked was to have a considerable effect upon their operation. The amalgamation presented opportunities for re-organisation and restructuring, and indeed there followed a period of re-organisation in all of the companies. As has been shown more recently, there is a tendency to concentrate on the re-organisation to the detriment of the business itself. The railway companies managed to improve financially, despite the decline in receipts, because greater costs reductions arose from the re-organisations.

Competition from road traffic (both passenger and goods) started to affect rail operations. All of the companies diversified into this area to stem this problem. However, it was the least of their problems; pressure from customers prevented many useful cut-backs from being implemented (e.g. the rationalisation and closure of duplicate freight depots). This problem was not really resolved until after the Beeching re-organisation of the mid 1960s.

These factors combined to create a shortage of capital, which came to a head in 1929 due to the growing economic depression. Nationalisation once again started to be discussed. The Boscawen Commission suggested a Public Transport Trust co-ordinating all modes of transport on a non profit-making basis, in effect a controlled monopoly somewhat akin to that which emerged after the Second World War. What did emerge during the early 1930s was the nationalisation of London's urban transport systems to form London Transport.

1933 Nationalisation – Success of LPTB?

Crompton (1995) notes that the creation of the London Passenger Transport Board – under the title London Transport – "...was generally regarded as a success by both supporters and opponents of nationalisation". Relevant to the nationalisation debate was the fact that this was the first time that shareholders had been dispossessed in a compulsory manner. Compensation was given in the form of LPTB 'C' shares.

The LPTB shares were meant to pay 5% for the first two financial years after nationalisation, and 5.5% thereafter, but never achieved these expectations. The peak return on the shares was a 4.25% distribution for the financial year ended 30th June 1937. Commentators of the day suggested that these expectations were higher than could be justified by the circumstances of the time. Shareholders could have called in a receiver under the terms of the 1931 legislation after the results for the 1937-8 financial year. They met in December 1938 but could not make a decision. LPTB agreed to raise fares so that by the time of a further shareholders meeting in early 1939 a 'wait-and-see' attitude was taken. The war had intervened by the time further results were reported, making receivership out of the question.

The poor LPTB results in 1938-9 were due to increasing costs and lower traffic growth; further fares increases were implemented. Whilst nationalisation had not delivered the expected financial returns to investors, London's travelling public had gained through the co-ordination of transport services in the capital. This co-ordination was further assisted by the programme of new works initiated between 1935 and 1940 (see below). The question of whether London Transport and its railway system remain in the public sector has again come to the fore, with the Conservatives offering in their 1997 election manifesto to privatise London Underground, if returned for a fifth term in office.

Investment in Railways and the 1935-40 New Works Programme

As noted above, the general economic situation and competitive pressures caused the railways to suffer a shortage of capital. Commentators such as Feinstein (1965), Aldcroft (1968) and

Crompton (1995) have suggested that one way of examining the railways' investment record was through their use of capital e.g. in electrification. Feinstein estimated that, over the period 1920-38, there was an average net disinvestment in the railways systems of £6.95 million p.a.

Studies commissioned throughout the 1920s (e.g. Merz & McLellan for the LNER, LMS and GWR) had shown that main line electrification could bring significant benefits in terms of operational performance. The financial returns quoted, however, were less spectacular:

- 7.2% on a capital outlay of £8.6m for the LNER (1931);
- 2.5% for the LMS (1931); and
- 0.75% for the GWR (1938).

Whilst some electrification schemes were implemented, they were generally only for suburban lines (e.g. Manchester – Altrincham). Only the Southern continued to undertake major network electrification, in the face of heavy competition from other modes. By accident rather than design, the Southern uncovered the phenomenon later called 'the sparks effect', which generated demand from improvements in service reliability and speed, and the regularisation of the timetable.

A study by Butterfield (1986) noted that the LNER were, by the mid 1920s, "...looking for Government assistance to undertake projects it certainly wished to proceed with ... for the simple reason that the company could not afford (innovation) unless the rewards were significant and certain". The certainty did not come until 1935, under a Government-sponsored programme.

The New Works Programme of 1935-40 was designed to alleviate unemployment. Under its auspices, the LPTB, along with the LNER and GWR, planned and constructed extensions and electrification using £40 million guaranteed by the Government. Schemes included:

- Electrification of the LNER from Liverpool Street – Shenfield;
- Extension of the Central line in tube from London Liverpool Street to Leytonstone, and the operation of

Central trains over the electrified Loughton branch and Fairlop loop;
- Extension of the Northern line from Highgate to East Finchley, and construction of a connection with the LNER at Finsbury Park, to enable tube trains to run on electrified tracks to Edgware, High Barnet and Alexandra Palace;
- Reconstruction of King's Cross, Post Office and a number of other central area stations.

Finance for the schemes was raised through a finance company specifically set up for the purpose. Croome and Jackson (1993) noted that "The Treasury guarantee was confirmed by a government measure – and the (LT) Board obtained powers to borrow from the finance company in the London Passenger Transport (Finance) Act 1935". There was no suggestion that any of the schemes were not financially viable; nevertheless, the Government guarantee on the bonds that were issued has always been of importance. The onset of the Second World War stopped all of the schemes. Some were completed afterwards, but some were curtailed and others abandoned altogether.

The New Works stand in marked contrast to the investment levels over the "Big Four" period. Analysis presented by Aldcroft (1968) suggests a significant disinvestment over the period 1920-38 of £125 million. This, coupled with the disinvestment that occurred during both wars, indicates the magnitude and source of the problems which British Railways faced subsequently, problems not addressed until the modernisation plan.

Competition and Co-ordination

Recent analysis has shown the significant rise in road vehicles between 1920 and 1939 (Helm, 1997). Goods vehicles rose by more than four times over the period, whilst private cars and vans rose tenfold (see Table 2.1). This growth in traffic had severely affected the ability of the railways to respond competitively. Road transport was unregulated until the Road Traffic Act of 1930, whilst railways were heavily regulated. Such differences remain to this day e.g. railways still have more stringent safety precautions than do road vehicle operators.

There is Nothing New in Railways!

Year	Private cars and vans	Buses, coaches and taxis	Goods Vehicles	Other Vehicles	TOTAL
1904	8	5	4	0	18
1913	106	39	64	98	306
1920	187	75	101	288	650
1930	1056	101	348	768	2274
1939	2034	90	488	536	3149
% growth 1920-39	52	1	20	5	20

Table 2.1 Road Traffic Growth 1904-39
(Source: Helm, 1997)

The major theoretical arguments of the 1930s were not in terms of nationalisation, but coordination. This implied that traffic should be moved on the mode which imposed the least level of social costs. Unfortunately, as Helm noted, this did not occur in practice because the Railways Act 1921 had imposed eight significant obligations on railways:

- to publish fares and charges;
- to act as a common carrier;
- to afford 'reasonable facilities';
- to facilitate through traffic;
- to show no undue preference;
- to provide reduced rate fares for workmen and the armed forces;
- to submit to statutory regulation of wages and working conditions; and
- to present returns and accounts to Government in a prescribed manner.

Road operators were not under such a burden, and could provide services based on cost, rather than on the classification system according to their value. Even in the 1930s, the railways felt that road operators were being subsidised through not having to pay their full costs, a situation which still applies today. The Road and Rail Traffic Act 1933 relaxed some of the burdens by allowing the railways to negotiate contracts on an individual basis. However, such contracts required the support of the Railway Rates Tribunal. Helm notes that only 850 approvals had been made by 1939, representing a gross turnover of only £4 million.

Technical innovation was also important, helping to reduce road transport costs by around a third over the period. Innovation did occur in the railways too, but low returns on investment did not enable the companies to acquire diesel or electric traction widely.

The railways did establish their own road goods vehicle fleets (to assist in the distribution of goods) and buses (through the purchase of, or acquiring interests in, bus companies). Aldcroft (1968) argues that the money invested in road transport would have better been spent on improving rail facilities, on the basis that the investment did not curb the competition. How the wheel has turned! Currently, it is the large bus companies who are acquiring rail franchises.

Railway receipts fell in 1938, affected by world economic conditions. The railways collaborated in launching the 'Square Deal' campaign aimed at removing the obligations noted above. They argued that they the obligations were no longer necessary and that, by removing them, they could compete more equitably with road transport. The 'Square Deal' was promoted as a contribution towards transport coordination, but the war intervened and the opportunities to carry it out did not arise.

The Second World War

The build-up to the war was very clear, and this enabled a relatively easy change to Government control, with management through the Railway Executive Committee. Whilst initially the railways were still operated as the four groups, by the end of 1941 they operated as a unified system. Significant spare capacity that had existed prior to the war was now in full use, and because of bombing, a system of alternative routes was implemented. This, coupled with improvements in wagon utilisation, and the deterrence of passenger travel, ensured that trains were available to carry the military and supplies necessary to support the war.

The Government agreed to support the railways financially throughout the war period, and that arrangement lasted until the railways were finally nationalised in 1948. The situation was different to that which had pertained in the first world war, since the railways were incentivised to assist the war effort through the revenue pooling schemes operated. The railways were thus able to earn large profits. However, as soon as the war ceased, traffic declined very sharply, causing similar acute financial problems to those which had plagued the railways after the first war.

Aftermath

Although the railways functioned adequately during the war, the neglect of maintenance began to show towards the end. Rolling stock had been intensively used and little maintained. Estimates put the total war damage and disinvestment at around £200 million. In order to address this, fares and charges needed to be raised to meet the increase in costs that had occurred. However, the increased granted could only go so far, given the greater threat from competing modes.

Planning for after the war began before it had finished. According to Bonavia (1980), staff at the Ministry of War Transport (as the Ministry of Transport had become) considered a wide range of organisational structures incorporating a "public control board", whilst stopping short of a "full-scale blueprint for railway nationalisation".

The incoming Labour Government of July 1945 gave its Minister of Transport the remit to nationalise the railways. The success of the co-ordination approach of London Transport was felt to be an appropriate model, and fitted the approach that Labour wanted to follow. Labour wished to, in the words of Clause 4, "secure for the workers by hand or by brain the full fruits of their industry and the most equitable distribution thereof that may be possible upon the cases of the common ownership of the means of production, distribution and exchange, and the best obtainable system of popular administration and control of each industry or service". Apart from Clause 4 and a document produced in the 1930s (the Labour Party, 1932), however, there was little to suggest how the task of nationalisation should be accomplished.

Railway Nationalisation

However, much work had been done during the war on the ways in which transport (and, indeed, urban areas) should be *re-planned* after the war. Even before the end of the war, the Ministry had commissioned and published a rail plan for London. This had fed off the outputs contained in the County of London Plan, which was the master plan for London to be achieved in the post-war period.

Given the poor state of the railways in 1945, nationalisation was inevitable. However, that did not prevent the companies from trying to stop it. The LMS, GWR and Southern had already ordered prototype diesel locomotives, and had some of them in service prior to nationalisation, whilst the LNER and Southern had operated electric locomotives prior to, and during, the war. Their (mainly negative) responses to nationalisation were put forward only when the Transport Bill was published. However, Bonavia (1980) highlights the constructive suggestion of the LNER whereby the nationalisation would be restricted to infrastructure. Under the 'landlord and tenant scheme' "the company would sell its track, structures, stations, etc., to the state and be granted a lease to operate train services on the payment of a rental for the use of the transferred assets. The purchase price would be used thoroughly to modernise the equipment, traction and rolling stock remaining with the Company". Although this process had been used in Italy and elsewhere, this close forerunner of the 1993 proposals was not taken up.

Indeed, all protestations were to no avail. British Railways was created as a nationalised company on 1st January 1948. Bonavia suggests that, had the Labour Government not come to power, then the railways would not have been nationalised. The compensation due would have afforded the rehabilitation of the systems, and the greater commercial freedom obtained from the 'square deal' campaign might have given a few years' breathing space before the post-war expansion of road transport took place at the end of the 1950s.

Nevertheless, the aftermath of war and the failure to invest led to other modes acquiring a competitive advantage over the railways. Coupled with the failure of the market to reflect true prices, perhaps railway nationalisation was indeed inevitable. However, Jenkins (1995) notes that "The private-sector companies that had been grouped in the 1921 Act were now in public ownership, but this merely altered the reporting line of their general managers". In other words, perhaps change was less far-reaching than it appeared. This is certainly also true in a number of cases in the privatisation of the 1990s.

Summary

This historical summary has sought to highlight a number of key points relating to Britain's railways in both public and private hands. Investment by the private sector has been a problem in the past, with Governments having to intervene. However, under-investment has also occurred when the railways have been under direct control. Market failure (in terms of prices not reflecting costs across the different transport modes) is an issue which still remains; the current outcome is severe road traffic congestion. The lessons of previous times need to be taken on board.

The Labour Party's ideological approach to nationalisation in the 1940s was based on very little substantive work, merely clause 4 of their constitution, a paper on the National Planning of Transport, and the operational success of London Transport. Similarly, there was relatively little in the way of policy debate in the privatisation of British Railways in the 1990s. BR existed as a nationalised industry, other privatisations had been successful, and all that was required was the right formula to sell it off.

Even in these few pages, then, we can see historical precedent for many of the current debates. Perhaps there is indeed nothing new in railways.

3 British Rail 1973 – 1983

There are a number of reasons for starting our detailed examination of the history of privatisation in 1973. First, British Railways as a nationalised industry was 25 years old. Secondly, several excellent modern histories were written up to this date (Bonavia, 1980; Gourvish, 1986), the latter of which was commissioned by the British Railways Board. Perhaps the most important reason for starting at this date, however, was that the route to privatisation can be seen to stem from the industrial unrest of the period.

New Government and a new Approach to the Railways

The political scene of 1973 bears some resemblance to that of 1997. The Labour Party, in opposition, had attacked the approach of the Heath Conservative Government as being mean. The 1974 Railways Act, passed by the incoming Labour administration, however, was an important turning point for British Rail. Three key elements emerged from this act:

1. a further financial reconstruction of BR;
2. a move towards a block grant structure for socially-necessary passenger rail services;
3. the introduction of grants to assist the provision of facilities for freight haulage by rail.

Although the 1968 Transport Act had brought some stability to railway finances, problems still existed. The 1974 Act wrote off £250 million of accumulated debt. Subsequent years saw a marginal improvement, with direct rail revenues exceeding direct rail expenditure. However, the past accumulation of debt continued to produce a net loss, except in 1977. The external economic situation made matters worse. Inflation increased for most of the period, and impacted on labour agreements.

Electrification

In terms of railway operation this period was something of a watershed in terms of railway operations. The completion of the electrification of the West Coast Main Line from London to Glasgow had a major impact on the cost efficiency of the route (e.g. locomotive changes were avoided and journey times were reduced from six hours to just over five hours). Indeed, the whole question of electrification of the railways again came to the fore. British Rail put forward considerable arguments about the need to keep electrification teams together and, to a certain extent, this was achieved through the development of a number of projects. However, the projects were (with two exceptions) quite limited in their scope (e.g. small infill projects such as Witham to Braintree). The two major projects of the period were the Great Northern Suburban Electrification (King's Cross & Moorgate – Royston) and the Bedford – St Pancras scheme.

A review of Main Line Electrification was published in 1981 (DoT/BRB, 1981). The report had followed a long line of such studies stretching back to the 1920's (1922, 1927, 1931, 1951, 1955 & 1978). Each report had concerned itself with the type and standardisation of electrification systems (e.g. voltage), and the costs and justification for such systems. Each succeeded in taking the idea and practice of electric railways forward, but none had ever been fully implemented within the planned timescale of the report.

The 1978 report (BRB, 1978) was produced as a discussion paper in which the BR Board set out a justification for a major enlargement of the electrified rail network, based on financial criteria. The document raised concerns about the methods of assessment used to determine the merits (or otherwise) of complex investment strategies required to achieve the expansion of the electrified network. BR did not have a comprehensive framework for evaluating such investments, nor did they have access to mathematical models through which they might have carried out Cost-Benefit Analysis or other such techniques. The pressure group Transport 2000, however, called for the used of CBA to achieve comparability between road and rail investment (Hamer, 1979).

Whilst some of the later reports had been costed, the 1981 report was able for the first time to analyse comprehensively the costs of a number of options and set financial benefits against the options. This enabled a *financial* cost benefit analysis to be performed and measured against a known base option. However, this excluded any wider "social" benefits arising from more traffic using rail, e.g. reductions in road traffic pollution, accidents, etc.

The main findings of the study, on the assumptions made, were "...a substantial programme of main line electrification would be financially worthwhile. All the larger electrification options examined show an internal rate of return of about 11%; the faster options give the higher net present values." The study carried out a wide of sensitivity tests, including looking at the effects of lower traffic forecasts and higher costs. Even if an unfavourable set of circumstances arose, the study report indicated that the financial return would be at least 7%. The study indicated to Government that the report was not a programme for main line electrification but a request for a "strategic decision in principle" to be taken. The report suggested that if the strategic decision were taken there were three arguments for going further and committing "to a specific programme":

1 Moving to a committed programme, rather than the previous ad hoc arrangements, would help to avoid abortive expenditure, and would secure cost reductions through steady production; it should also improve the competitiveness of the UK rail electrification industry.
2 It would give BRB a firmer basis for its financial plans. The electrification programme would require up to £60 million per year in cash flow and such requirements would exceed the investment ceiling set by the Government.
3 The benefits of individual projects cannot be evaluated without judgments concerning the extent of a future electrified network, otherwise decisions concerning investment would be distorted.

Many of the arguments and studies addressed by the study had been aired in the years before the study was undertaken. However, the report was a watershed in setting out the level of financial support required for a modern railway to be developed. It was important in helping a Conservative Government realise that it could not afford such a capital programme.

Corporate blue livery, before Sectorisation, privatisation or electrification of cross-city services: a DMU leaves Birmingham New Street [E.W. Godward]

Problem Lines

Throughout this decade, the issue of "Problem Lines" emerged. Following the passage of the Transport Act 1968, the costs of support for operations on unprofitable lines had been identified. Richard Marsh, who had been Minister of Transport in the late 1960s, and was then Chairman of the BRB from 1971-1976, stated in his autobiography (Marsh, 1978, p. 165):

"In 1968 I had been for seeing on to the Statute Book a major Transport Act which had, among other things, wiped out British Rail's capital debts of £1200 million, and had given them yet another new start. In 1969 and 1970, as a result of these massive capital write-offs, British Rail had claimed to make profits, but they had, in fact, only been making surpluses. They certainly had not been generating a sufficiently large surplus to replace their assets, and it did not take me very long, after arriving at the Board, to see that once again we were sliding back into the red."

Marsh notes that it was not a case of incompetent management; every major passenger rail operator had problems of unbalanced finances. A top level exercise was therefore set up to determine whether there were profitable networks. To minimise the losses the exercise suggested the need for a large increase in investment, with even the least profitable network requiring an investment programme of £1800 million. In order to achieve this, however, network closures would be required – largely in rural and Conservative-voting areas.

The 1950s had seen the developments of costing systems for rail routes. Accurate (if primitive and manual) allocation of revenues and charges allowed the railways to see whether routes were or were not remunerative. These highlighted the problems of routes such as the Cambrian Coast, or Haltwhistle-Alston. However, Government was unwilling to accept the BR argument wholesale. They were not prepared to "identify the level of acceptable loss and stop pretending that it can produce a commercial return". The Department of Transport therefore commissioned research into whether rail routes could be converted into busways. The research, when published however, was much derided (Glover, 1985). Academics and the public began to see a wider role for the railways (Hamilton & Potter, 1985; Railway Invigoration Society, 1977).

Prestige Projects

During the period, the railways attempted to pursue a number of prestigious projects, including the Channel Tunnel and its associated rail links, and the development of high speed traction to challenge both air and road competition.

The Channel Tunnel and its associated rail links: The planning of a tunnel linking Britain and France has been ongoing since 1802, but renewed proposals for both the tunnel and rail links to it were developed in the early 1970s. Many of the technical details of the Channel Tunnel Rail Link route were published in 1972. The BR route differed from those developed by consultant engineers, largely by following the line of existing rail corridors. In 1973 the Heath Government produced a White Paper in which it was accepted that "the full potential of the 'Chunnel' could only be realised by simultaneous development of high speed rail links."

However, it was revealed in 1974 that the cost of the CTRL project had risen from £120 million to £373 million (excluding land acquisition, compensation and environmental costs). As a result, Harold Wilson's Government put the project on hold, and it was abandoned in early 1975 due to more general fiscal problems. The project remained dormant until the early 1980s. The proposal to build the Channel Tunnel in its current form was revived in 1981, by BR and their French counterparts at SNCF. It assumed a high-speed rail link between London and the tunnel portal, along the lines of the French "Lignes a Grande Vitesse". For both capital financing and planning reasons, it made a great deal of sense to tie the construction of the new line to the build-up of international traffic through the tunnel. The story of the Channel Tunnel has been set out by, amongst others, Wilson (1991), whilst the rail link is only now being developed.

Faster Trains: The development of high-speed passenger railways in the UK has been a typical 'on-off' affair. The move towards higher speeds started during the 1920s, when competition from the car first started to affect rail patronage. Three of the four main railway companies developed higher-speed services.

From the mid 1960s, the airline industry started to operate jet aircraft on regular services. In 1971, changes in aircraft technology led to the development of hub airports, further weakening the competitiveness of rail over longer distances. Rail was relegated to serving intermediate points between main airports. Developments such as electrification, whilst serving to increase the competitiveness of rail between these intermediate points, could only make a small impact on the longer distance markets. What was required was to bring rail into the market where it could be competitive, and this required that services should be significantly speeded up.

The re-emergence of rail came about through the ability to create mass markets. The limitations of aircraft technology meant that it was not sensible to operate very large aircraft on domestic routes. Unlike the French Railways, who had built a dedicated high-speed line, BR's developments showed how rail could higher speeds on existing tracks.

Two parallel projects for higher-speed traction were undertaken. One was to develop existing rail, suspension and traction technology. This led to the diesel-powered High Speed Train entering service in 1976; it made a significant improvement to both the passenger comfort and the finances of long-distance rail travel. Advances in rail technology, plus inputs from the airline industry, allowed the development of the tilting Advanced Passenger Train. This underwent considerable development, with both gas turbine and electric power, but the project was not successful, and was terminated in 1986. Williams (1985) suggested that the failure of the APT was due to a number of reasons including:

(i) prolonged under-investment in railways in the UK;

(ii) too many untried technical innovations on one trains; and

(iii) a lack of engineering understanding of the requirements of tilting trains.

*The Prestige Project that failed:
the Advanced Passenger Train (APT) [E.W. Godward]*

However, various technological spin-offs were used in subsequent designs of train, and the tilting mechanism presaged a more widespread use of tilt internationally.

The APT was intended to operate on the West Coast main line route. With its failure, developments in high-speed running switched to other major routes, including the Great Western Main Line (where HSTs have been in squadron service for 15 years) and the East Coast Main Line (ECML).

A study by Allen et al (1977) showed that rail speeds on the ECML have risen consistently since the 1960s. First, the route used high-speed 'Deltic' diesel locomotives hauling conventional coaches. Upon life expiry, these were replaced initially by HSTs, and then by Class 91 electric locomotives hauling semi-permanently-coupled sets of coaches. These included Driving Van Trailers to achieve higher utilisation, by reducing turn-round times. With a top speed of 225km/hr, these trains incorporate some APT technology, and are amongst the most cost-effective trains in the world. They have played a key role in developing the profitability of the East Coast route.

The introduction of new trains has often been dogged by problems associated with the technology. On BR, a further problem arose as productivity improvements led to problems with industrial relations.

The Nettle of Productivity

The issue of productivity came to dominate policy at the end of the 1970s. The number of staff employed by the BRB fell by over 20% between 1974 and 1983, from 199,437 to 155,423. This continued a drive towards a more productive railway, ongoing since nationalisation; British Railways had employed 648,740 staff at the end of 1948. This drive had been pursued with more or less vigour by the Board and by Government, dependent upon the state of BR's financial performance, as well as the state of national finances. The description of the processes is given very clearly by Richard Marsh, who was unique in serving as both Minister of Transport and then Chairman of British Rail. He said of the unions and Government (1978): "Successive Governments have sought to use the unions as an excuse and a whipping boy for their own incompetence and failure to face up to problems which are contrary to the pictures Ministers try to paint".

He draws an awkward picture of the 'stop-go' situation that faced the railways in improving productivity:

> "You frequently employ more people than you need in theory, because in the real world of cuts in investment and expensive redundancy schemes you cannot afford to get rid of them. There is no reason for employing a single level-crossing attendant anywhere in Britain, for example. All that has to be done is to put in automatic half-barrier level crossings but Governments then cancel the capital investment monies which would have done just that."

Peter Parker, who followed Richard Marsh as Chairman in 1976, felt that British Rail had succeeded in improving some of the above Government/BR failings through the setting of clear objectives. Parker (1989) states that the price of "…victory for electrification was unconvincing at that stage; it could only be done if 38,000 jobs were shed from the system." In order to achieve that, significant changes in working practices would be required, including single-manning and flexible rostering. In addition to the normal tensions between management and unions, there were also inter-union problems. These were compounded by a personality clash between Sid Weighell, the General Secretary of the NUR (National Union of Railwaymen) and Ray Buckton, with a similar position at ASLEF (Associated Society of Locomotive Enginemen and Firemen).

In 1981, according to Parker, there was a "widely acclaimed pay and productivity settlement." The six specific items sought by the BR Board were:

- fewer staff in the cabs of freight trains;
- fewer staff in the cabs of passenger trains;
- open stations;
- the introduction of the trainperson concept, to open up career prospects of becoming either a driver or a conductor;
- one-person operation of certain trains; and
- flexible rostering.

Flexible rostering proved to be the major stumbling block, although some of the other issues (e.g. one-person operation) also gave problems, and caused trains to remain idle in sidings for long periods. Flexible rostering was designed to overcome the problem of the inflexibility of rigid eight hour shifts, which had resulted in low driver productivity, with average useful driving times of only three hours 20 minutes. It gave variable shift lengths within certain limits. The net result was to give employees a shorter working week, more rest days and fewer shifts requiring starts during the middle of the night.

BR were reluctant to offer more than a minimal increase in pay without the clear acceptance of the agreed specifics of productivity being accepted and implementation begun. This caused strikes. BR's position toughened; they threatened to withdraw the pay increase if the principles were not accepted. The matter was referred to a tribunal which, after a long deliberation, came down unequivocally for BR and the commitments which ASLEF had already agreed to. Militant members of the NUR threatened to strike.

Peter Parker, as Chairman of BR, wrote to all workers at their home addresses twice indicating the gravity of their actions if they chose to strike: no pay increase, the prospect of no job for many, and no prospect of electrification investment. Some union members saw the hand of the Thatcher Government at work, but Parker states that this was not the case. (He himself was left-leaning in politics, and had stood as a Labour candidate in the 1951 election.) ASLEF began their strike on the 4th July 1982.

The BR Board held its nerve. This, along with clear communication of the issues, led to the resolution of the strike after the intervention of the Trade Union Congress and the Government's Arbitration, Conciliation and Advisory Service (ACAS). The strike damaged BR, but not irreparably.

The Serpell Report

Between 1975 and 1982, the deficit on railway operations rose from £692 million to £1,035 million (before any grants and payment of interest). Concern over this deteriorating financial position led the Government to Commission a major study of Railway Finances. This was initiated in 1982 and was chaired by Sir David Serpell. The adage "what goes around comes around" was very apposite. In his younger days Serpell had been Deputy Secretary in the Department of Transport involved in railway policy formation in the Marples – Beeching era.

The main aims of the study were:
1. to assess the current financial position of the railways;
2. to assess the extent to which the financial position of the railways could be improved within existing policies, and
3. what might be achieved by major changes or departures from those policies.

Its key conclusions were that there were *"many opportunities to improve efficiency and reduce costs of the railway while keeping it at broadly its present size."* However, it is not generally remembered for that conclusion, but rather for its network scenarios. Although the study was time-constrained, it looked at five options against the base, in order to assess whether significant economic improvements might arise from a smaller network. In mileage terms the five options were as follows:

option	mileage
Base 1983	10541
A	1630
B	2220
C1	10461
C2	8781
C3	6120

Essentially, Serpell can be considered as unfinished. No proper assessment of the full resource costs were carried out, nor was a cost:benefit exercise conducted to assess the overall effects. The network effects not understood by Beeching were largely not examined here either – for instance, what would the impact be on the lines from Glasgow and Edinburgh to England if there was no network North of these cities? However, the report, and the dissenting minority report by Alfred Goldstein, did strike a chord with some in the Government. It is true to say that, financially, the railways would not be where they are today had it not been for this study. It emphasised the continuing requirement for subsidy merely to operate the railway. Taken with the Electrification Report's conclusions about capital funding, Serpell laid the seeds for a Government wishing to rid itself of an industry needing so much public money. Wider transport policy issues were not considered.

Summary

The decade 1973-1983 can be characterised by a small number of themes, in particular investment and productivity. BR became more efficient, even if losing traffic. Prestige projects such as the Channel Tunnel and high-speed traction power, together with the Review of Main Line Electrification demonstrated a continuing requirement for government capital. Problems with rural lines and ongoing financial problems, highlighted by the Serpell Report, demonstrated a continuing need for government subsidy. These two reports were critical in shaping the views of a Conservative Government opposed to state support for the rail industry. In addition, the strikes cast a shadow over the railways as a nationalised industry.

4 British Rail 1984-1994

This chapter sets out the progress British Rail made in its last 10 years before privatisation. Although the 10-year period was broadly divided into five rich years and five lean years, treatment of the subject solely in this manner would fail to observe some of the longer-term changes affecting the railway industry, which are described in their own sections below.

The Economic Boom 1984 -1989

During the mid 1980s, Britain was relatively prosperous. A Conservative Government led by Mrs Thatcher and committed to tax cuts was in power; in 1987 the then Chancellor, Nigel Lawson, injected a very large amount of money into the economy through personal reductions in income tax. As it turned out, this injection of spending power turned out to be too large; the economy subsequently overheated and plunged into recession.

In the good years, however, economic activity went from strength to strength, and the railways fared reasonably well too (see Figure 4.1). Traffic levels were buoyed up by the economy; businesses could afford to send employees first class, which maintained InterCity receipts, whilst individuals could afford days out and weekends away, which sustained high levels of offpeak traffic. Conditions on Britain's roads worsened as congestion became endemic in many areas and, for the first time, even on some of the motorways, including the newly-opened M25. On the freight side, even the staple industries which provided the backbone of every railway's freight operations were declining more slowly than they had been (see Figure 4.1 again).

Although the railways' market share was continuing to fall, traffic was rising slightly. In some places, the strain on the Victorian infrastructure was noticeable. In the South Wales Valleys (Davies & Clark, 1996) and in London, demand rose

British Rail 1984 – 1994

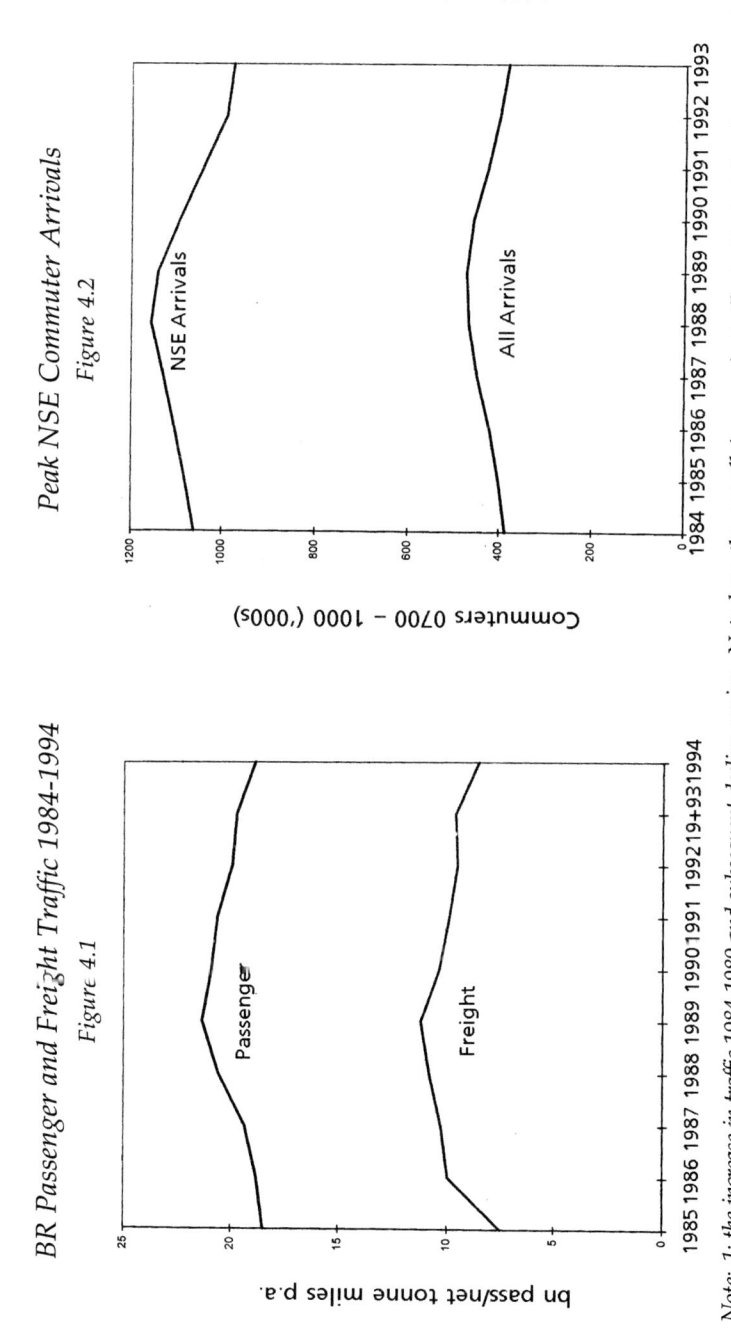

Peak NSE Commuter Arrivals
Figure 4.2

Note how the overall increase in traffic to Central London was met almost entirely by increases in the numbers of commuters carried by rail.

BR Passenger and Freight Traffic 1984-1994
Figure 4.1

Note: 1: the increase in traffic 1984-1989 and subsequent decline again; 2: the so-called boom added only around 10% to traffic levels, but much of this was sheer profit.

significantly. Peak commuter arrivals in London reached their maximum in 1989, exceeding the levels of the early 1960s (see Figure 4.2). Standing became part of the game for NSE commuters. This led to political pressure, which in turn led to Government action in terms of the Central London Rail Study (DTp et al, 1989). This report recommended significant improvements to London's railway network for both LUL and NSE services, including East – West Crossrail, a new RER-type line linking suburban services out of Liverpool Street (in the East) and Paddington and Marylebone (in the West).

Boom time: Commuters crowd the platforms at London Bridge [N.G. Harris]

Sector Management

It was during the 1980s that BR began to develop organisationally into a modern railway. One man in particular was instrumental in this development – Bob Reid I. Sir Bob, an ex-LNER trainee appointed to the BR chairmanship, understood the environment in which the railway would have to operate in the future. Dominance by engineers was not an option. Railways must be run along business lines, with middle management aware of the costs and revenues attributable to the services which they were responsible for.

Aware that a full and immediate change to such a regime would be too much for the industry to cope with, 1982 saw the setting-up of sectors to lead the business side of the railway. Five sectors were set up – InterCity, London & SouthEast, Other Provincial, Freight and Parcels. Within each of these, lines of route or groups of services were managed individually e.g. the East Coast Main Line within the InterCity business. Ongoing improvements in marketing, service promotion and cost control continued the commercialisation of the railways, and brought about significant changes in financial performance. A new culture of customer care began to be developed in the outer reaches of the network, including Cornwall and Scotland (Stewart & Chadwick, 1987).

The management structure was a matrix structure, with regionally-organised operations departments providing the services specified and paid for by the businesses (Cochrane, 1992). Regions soon found themselves dealing with more than one sector, and internal trading agreements were set up. For instance, Norwich Crown Point depot looked after InterCity trains operating out of Liverpool Street, as well as rolling stock for local Provincial services in East Anglia.

Fares Policy

Although systematic manipulation of the fares structure had occurred as long ago as the mid 1960s, it was only really in the 1980s that fares policy began to be used in earnest both to raise revenue and control costs. Each of the passenger sectors saw that they had offpeak capacity, whilst they could not afford to reduce fares across-the-board, since captive travellers (e.g. in the business and commuter markets) were often prepared to pay more.

In the mid 1980s, a new national fares structure developed, with "ordinary" tickets being reduced to a minority. The most common tickets for travel were the day return (for local travel, and generally limited to avoiding the commuter peaks in the urban areas) and the Saver (for longer-distance journeys, and restricted to those trains avoiding the key business services to and from London). Reduced-rate travel in the peaks was only generally available to season ticket holders. In such a manner, the demand for travel was managed in the peaks (even if congestion levels were sometimes unacceptable) and hence capacity not well-used was not installed. These policies of market segmentation were developed considerably throughout the decade, as increasingly-technical analysis was carried out (Fowkes & Nash, 1991; Harris, 1992c), and undoubtedly helped maximise revenue whilst minimising costs.

InterCity into profit

Successive Governments had desired to offer no subsidy to long-distance transport in Britain. After only a short period of operation, this was the task set for the InterCity sector, a task which seemed Herculean at the time. In 1984, InterCity made a loss of over £100m (20% on its bottom line). Sector Directors Cyril Bleasdale and then John Prideaux were set the task of turning the business round.

The plan to bring InterCity into profit had four elements (Glover, 1985). First, the sector was to be redefined. For example, Waterloo – Bournemouth services were removed from the sector's portfolio, whilst the London – Norwich service was added. Over time, a few other parts of the IC network in Britain were also lost – such as Barrow, Blackpool and Cleethorpes. Secondly, costs were to be cut through improved resource management (e.g. better rolling stock utilisation). Thirdly, as we have seen, a new fares strategy aimed to relate prices nearer to production costs. Lastly, revenue was to rise through product reshaping (e.g. the improvement of ancillary services such as seat reservations and catering).

Indeed, those who worried about cost savings driving the InterCity changes should not have been. In fact, some of the actions taken increased cost – but added more value. Foremost amongst these was the reintroduction of Pullman services on the key business routes. Pullman service was expensive, but a package of good food, seat reservations and free parking at stations was attractive to business customers, many of whom became regulars.

The completion of the ECML electrification in 1991 was the highlight of the InterCity sector (Semmens, 1991). New trains,

British Rail 1984 – 1994

InterCity: High Speed Train at Dawlish [N.G. Harris]

Network SouthEast: Class 455 no.5827 arrives at East Dulwich [N G Harris]

140mph running, frequent services (Newcastle, 270 miles from London, had a half-hourly service for large parts of the day) and electric haulage replacing diesel, saw revenues rise (both in volume terms, and in rates per mile) whilst operating costs fell. It was undoubtedly the star financial performer of the long-distance routes.

The NSE dream

The London & South East sector was primarily a commuter rail business. It adopted the so-called "Jaffa Cake" livery of browns and oranges but after around a year, it was relaunched under the charismatic leadership of Chris Green, its new director.

On 10 June 1986 one train on each main radial route was presented to the public in the new Network SouthEast colours of blue white and red – colours deliberately designed to appeal to the region's predominantly Conservative voters. As a marketing stunt designed to bring together a number of disparate operations, lamp-posts were painted bright red all over the Network, within a matter of days. A positive aura was brought about.

In 1982, London Transport introduced cheaper and zonally-based fares, which were subject to a legal challenge by the London Borough of Bromley in 1983, but which formed the basis for a revised initiative including NSE as well as London Transport. Capitalcards (introduced in January 1985) enabled BR commuters to travel cheaply at other times on underground and bus services in the capital; these tickets were subsequently merged with LT's similar Travelcards. These measures probably added some 20% to peak rail flows just as employment in Central London's booming financial services economy added a further 30%. NSE management became very bullish, even suggesting that a subsidy-free Network was foreseeable.

The NSE network expanded. Using the disused Snow Hill tunnel, a scheme drawn up by GLC planners to link services North and South of the Thames was implemented. The Network truly was a network, and through journeys on "Thameslink" services between Bedford and Brighton became possible.

Sprinterisation and Regional reopenings

The management of "Other Provincial Services" soon decided that such a title was unmarketable, and they lost the "Other",

Thameslink: New cross-London services started on 29th May 1990, such as this one seen at Farringdon. [E.W. Godward]

subsequently rechristening themselves Regional Railways. In a railway business where costs typically outweighed farebox revenues by 4:1, cost reductions were clearly going to be of importance.

The Privatisation of British Rail

Fortunately for the railways, however, the strategy developed was generally a positive one. Although some network and service retrenchments were attempted (most notably the failed attempt to close the infamous Settle and Carlisle line (Abbott & Whitehouse, 1990)), costs were mostly to be reduced through investment. By the end of the 10-year period, the average age of Regional trains was only eight years. A series of new DMU designs was unveiled, ranging from the Class 14x railbuses to the 15x Sprinters. As the latter were introduced, specifications rose, so that the last batches included air-conditioning and had a 100mph capability. Although new two-car sets invariably replaced old three-car sets, longer vehicles and different seating arrangements were generally regarded as an improvement – except amongst a number of minority groups such as cyclists, since guards' vans were abolished.

Other parts of the Sprinterisation package included replacement of infrequent locomotive-hauled services with Sprinters. The Newcastle/Scarborough – Liverpool/North Wales service, previously providing an hourly service across the Pennines with seven-coach trains, was improved to every 20 minutes, albeit with two- and three-car services. However, the increased frequency, combined with a more modern ambience and trolley catering, brought significant increases in demand.

The last major part of the Sprinterisation package was the linking together of local services to create new markets, as passengers no longer had to change. Foremost amongst the new axes created was Liverpool – Norwich via Sheffield and Peterborough. New journey opportunities stimulated demand, whilst improving vehicle utilisation. The overall Regional operating ratio improved to 3:1.

In some cases, the rerouteing of services enabled further interchange opportunities to be developed. Railways in the Manchester area were significantly improved with the construction of the Windsor link, enabling trains from Preston to reach the two through platforms at Manchester Piccadilly and hence Stockport and the South of Manchester. Capacity for this to occur had been provided by Manchester's Metrolink tram services, which opened in 1992, taking over BR's Bury and

British Rail 1984 – 1994

*Regional Railways: A Class 141 in West Yorkshire PTE livery at York
[E.W. Godward]*

*From BR Network: Manchester Metrolink set 1015 at Altrincham
[N.G. Harris]*

Altrincham local services with great success (within a year, annual patronage was at 13 million passengers, compared to nine million when operated as separate local rail services).

Across the country, Regional Railways also participated in a large number of railway development schemes, often in partnership with the Passenger Transport Executives (the transport coordinating bodies of the Metropolitan counties). The leader in this field was West Yorkshire PTE, which was responsible for 18 new stations, although Greater Manchester, South Yorkshire and Merseyside also joined in (RDS, 1992). New planning methods were required to estimate demand for possible station sites and routes, and Leeds University were involved from the start (Preston, 1992). Most schemes were opened under the "Speller amendment", which permitted services to be operated on an experimental basis.

One of the most successful reopenings was that of the Bathgate branch in Central Scotland. Bathgate was an industrial town where recession had hit hard, and it had lost its passenger services in the 1960s. However, contributions from BR, Lothian Regional Council and the EEC, together with an agreement with the freight sector that they remained the prime user of the line, provided favourable conditions for new passenger services. Demand exceeded estimates by a wide margin, and over one million trips p.a. were being made on this branch within four years of its opening in March 1986.

If councils were not involved in railway development, property developers usually were. The growth of business parks and shopping supercentres in the late 1980s provided a number of opportunities for new stations, including at Winnersh Triangle (Berkshire), Gateshead MetroCentre (Tyne & Wear) and Meadowhall (South Yorkshire). Meadowhall, situated adjacent to the M1 and between the major centres of Sheffield and Rotherham, was constructed with a new station sited on the junction of the Sheffield-Barnsley and Sheffield-Doncaster lines. This prime position enabled a high level of service to be offered, and reasonable patronage levels accrued, despite a bus station and huge car-parking facilities also being available. In 1994, Sheffield's Supertram also reached Meadowhall, making it a

British Rail 1984 – 1994

*New lines: A Class 101 at Uphall,
on the Edinburgh – Bathgate line, opened 1985. [J.W.E. Rodley]*

Sheffield Supertram at Meadowhall [N.G. Harris]

genuine transport interchange. Rail transport has undoubtedly helped Meadowhall become a regional shopping centre.

New stations were also occasionally built with new housing developments, although many new housing estates unfortunately grew up away from existing stations. Hedge End, in Hampshire, was a new station built in 1990 on the Eastleigh – Fareham line to serve new local development.

New Stations: A VEP at Hedge End, Hampshire. [N.G. Harris]

Airport Links

In addition to the generally-local developments sponsored by Regional Railways, the BRB itself contributed significantly to two projects of national importance – the airport links to Stansted and Manchester airports. A total of £44.5m was spent on a new rail link to Stansted airport, reached by a single-track branch from the London Liverpool Street – Cambridge line. A new half-hourly shuttle service to London was launched, and garnered as much as 25% of airport traffic, but Stansted itself fared relatively poorly. Regional Railways services on the North-West – Cambridge axis were extended to the airport at first, but were cut back as the airport failed to develop as quickly as hoped.

British Rail 1984 – 1994

Airport Links: A Class 322 EMU at Stansted Airport. [N.G. Harris]

Manchester had a high profile in the early 1990s. As well as bidding as a site for both Olympic and Commonwealth Games, development at the airport continued, and a short double-track branch was opened off the Piccadilly – Heald Green line in 1993. With Sprinterisation of many Regional services and the rationalisation of services in Manchester noted above, the airport soon gained a wide range of services to key centres throughout the North of England, including Leeds, Preston and Middlesbrough.

Efficiency

Britain's railways made great strides in efficiency throughout the 1980s. Fewer and fewer resources were used to carry volumes of traffic which (especially on the passenger side) remained at roughly constant levels. All parts of the business contributed, and in all fashions. Administration was focussed more clearly with the development of business sectors (especially the second stage, of Organising for Quality (see below)). Minor network simplifications reduced overheads – for example through the diversion of traffic from Lincoln St Mark's to Lincoln Central. A few more powerful locomotives (e.g. the heavy freight classes 56, 58 and 60) replaced a larger number of smaller locos often used in multiple (e.g. classes 20, 25). The modernisation of the DMU fleet reduced maintenance requirements, and there were a significant number of depots closed, even in substantial provincial centres; examples included Hull Botanic Gardens, Bradford Hammerton Street, and Gateshead.

All these improvements fed through into the operating performance of the railways, and their impact could be seen in the Annual Report and Accounts (see Figure 4.3). However, the reduced availability of spare rolling stock meant that additional trains at peak periods gave way to higher prices at holiday weekends, and the non-availability of substitute trains when the booked services broke down. Crowding increased, as did the number of passenger complaints. However, with support from public funds at only 0.16% of GNP (as opposed to 0.52% in the rest of Western Europe (BRB, 1993)), the railway became to be admired professionally, as many foreign railway staff came to BR to see how railways could be run without vast subsidy.

Recession 1989-1994

Unfortunately for both BR and Britain as a whole, the boom years of the late 1980s gave way to the recession of the early 1990s. Transport being the derived demand that it is, the railways suffered considerably. Just as the BRB were agreeing to reduced Government subsidies, less favourable economic conditions were reducing their traffic income. First class passengers traded down to second class. Businesses sent fewer parcels – and fewer bulk goods. Fewer people had jobs – so fewer went to work. Peak arrivals on NSE services at London's termini fell by 100,000 to 350,000 over a three-year period, whilst it proved impossible to cut costs by this ratio. Reduced consumer confidence led to a reduction in offpeak journeys, which was particularly noticeable in the NSE area, where fewer service improvements were coming on stream.

The railway's financing requirements rose, but the Conservative Government contained influential right-wing politicians who favoured reducing public expenditure. Rail investment in the existing system suffered, with monies being spent on Channel Tunnel-related works and revenue support instead. A large road construction programme was developed,

BR Efficiency Gains 1984-1994 (Train Kilometres per Staff Member)
Figure 4.3

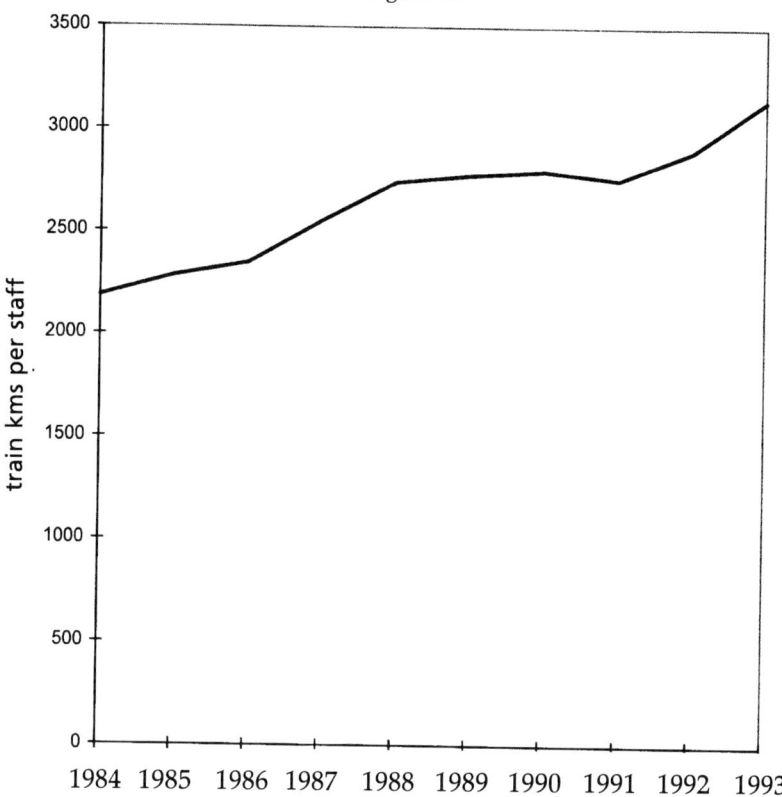

but public opinion was gradually turning away from the car, and the burgeoning national debt forced a reduction in the roads budget too. Meanwhile, road congestion continued to be a problem, especially on the motorways and in South East England; regret began to be expressed about some of the politically-driven railway closures of the Beeching era (Henshaw, 1991).

The run-down of the coal industry had a devastating impact on Trainload Freight. Annual tonnages of coal halved – and with them, much of TlF's profits. Colliery lines all over the country fell into disrepair as the newly-privatised electricity generators switched to gas. However, it was not all bad news as (probably subsidised) imported coal was also bought, and Railfreight was able to develop its links to some of the docks (notably Avonmouth and Liverpool) to carry some of this traffic. Moreover, the split of BR's Trainload freight business into three (Mainline, Loadhaul and Transrail) did provide the stimulus for some positive developments, and additional traffic was reclaimed from the roads. Significantly, Transrail developed one line of route for the wagonload business previously shunned by corporate BR; its Enterprise services carried traffic on an axis linking Cornwall, Warrington and Scotland.

Sale of subsidiaries

As part of an ongoing Government privatisation programme, BR was required to sell off its subsidiary companies. During the period, Sealink (shipping services, 1984), Travellers Fare (catering, 1988), BR Engineering Ltd. (1989), Meldon Quarry (ballast extractors) and Transmark (consultancy) were all either sold to competitors or as part of a Management Buy-Out. Not all of these had a trouble-free ride; Doncaster Works (privatised as RFS under an MBO) called in the receivers in late 1993 as a dearth of orders caused cash-flow problems.

OfQ and Preparation for Privatisation

During the recession, BR continued to grapple with its costs. In 1993, Bob Reid I's vision of a business-led railway finally came to pass, with the abolition of the matrix management structure and its replacement with Organising for Quality (OfQ). Under matrix management, sectors guided railway policy, but had contracts with operating and contracting units who respectively operated and maintained the railway. Under OfQ, however, all railway employees were now directly responsible to a director who had all his own costs and revenues, and made his own business decisions. The direct staff on InterCity's books jumped from 350 to 35,000 as they became responsible for all infrastructure maintenance on their routes, rather than merely contracting it from Regional Engineers. Investment was focussed on those areas producing the best returns, whilst costs were contained behind the scenes – especially in InterCity.

But just as these developments were being completed, the Government announced its plans for privatisation, in which contracting out was to be the order of the day. Train operators would no longer be responsible for infrastructure maintenance. The railway aimed for its highest – the 1994 timetable, a product of OfQ, was reckoned to be the best ever, although by the time it was introduced, OfQ had ended.

Total Route Modernisation

One of the ways in which investment was increasingly applied for the best returns was in the 'Total Route Modernisation' approach. Rather than spreading investment thinly, a policy was adopted of concentrating developments on particular corridors. Resignalling and track rationalisation were usually carried out hand-in-hand. Following an experiment at Crewe in 1985, passenger disruption during works was minimised by development of the "Big Bang" approach, in which lines were often closed completely, sometimes for several weeks, in order that expensive machinery might be used to the full. Not only were there some cost savings in doing infrastructure improvements jointly, but step changes in services were often possible. NSE's Chiltern lines were the first to benefit from such an approach. New trains, coupled with a new depot at Aylesbury and other infrastructure improvements, soon took the route from its Cinderella status within the commuter lines to one of the best.

Elsewhere in the country, Birmingham's Cross-City service was being electrified (Godward, 1987), and new trains provided, but delays with the latter took the sparkle off this package. Manchester's Metrolink, Airport and Sprinter services improved services in North West England by a quantum leap over a period of only a few years.

Investment

Overall, however, investment was generally limited. Although the Government constantly intimated that investment levels in the railways were higher than since the Modernisation Plan years of the

Total Route Modernisation: New Class 165 Turbos and new stabling point at Marylebone. [N.G. Harris]

1950s, the vast majority of this was in works related to the Channel Tunnel. The saga of the Channel Tunnel has been documented elsewhere (Wilson, 1991; Ridley, 1992) but the Tunnel itself, costing £10Bn, only constituted part of the story. A magnificent new station at Waterloo was finished on time in 1993, whilst wholesale track relaying of all routes to the Tunnel was completed in the period 1991-1993. Automation of procedures lead to new productivity records being broken, and track lengths relaid in a weekend were soon measured in kilometres rather than yards. Even last-minute technical hitches associated with relays upsetting high-tech equipment on the Eurostar trains failed to obliterate the achievement only really noticed by Kent commuters, who simultaneously were at last enjoying new Networker stock to replace their 1950-vintage EPBs.

Much to the dismay of Eurotunnel investors (but not, one assumes the ferry companies), the Tunnel opened over one year late, with freight shuttle, passenger shuttle and through passenger services beginning progressively through 1994. However, it was 1995 before the operation could be said to be fully underway.

The core of the InterCity network, the West Coast Main Line between London and Glasgow, continued to deteriorate, due to a lack of investment. Train reliability fell, whilst 1960s signalling equipment became outdated. The *InterCity 250* project was born, as an attempt to develop the line with a run-on order of Class 91 locomotives already provided for the parallel East Coast route, with improvements to infrastructure and signalling. However, the impetus for the project was lost due to the impending separation of Railtrack from BR's train operations, and the project stalled.

£150m of additional investment monies prised out of the Treasury during 1993 were subject to a competition between InterCity and NSE. Whilst InterCity needed pump-priming for investment in the West Coast route, NSE needed cash to replace further elderly multiple units falling apart, and it was the latter bid which won, largely on political grounds, with the money going on a leasing deal for 41 outer-suburban trains. The replacement of much of the WCML at a cost of up to £1bn remained a key problem for senior railway managers.

However, it was certainly not the only problem. Continuing neglect of non-visible infrastructure meant that significant problems were also apparent on the signalling side. This was not confined to large schemes (such as the resignalling of the lines out of Waterloo, at perhaps £250m), but a whole host of smaller schemes, some of which threatened line closures, such as of the Paddock Wood – Strood line in Kent (Ford, 1993b).

Elsewhere, funding problems meant that BR had to withdraw from the proposed fast link from London's Paddington station to Heathrow; fortunately for the other participant (British Airports Authority), a Japanese bank filled the gap vacated by BR.

Private Sector Involvement

In addition to the contracting out of services and the privatisation of subsidiaries, the private sector was becoming increasingly involved in the railways even before privatisation itself occurred. Leasing became an ever-more important way of financing assets,

Waterloo International. [N.G. Harris]

although Treasury restrictions on what constituted Public Sector borrowing sometimes thwarted apparently-sensible deals.

A major positive development was in the parcels business, where a new contract was negotiated with Royal Mail. This included the creation of a new network of routes for postal trains, together with new purpose-built electric multiple units, and a number of new terminals such as at Willesden (London) and Gateshead (Newcastle).

Whilst the Heathrow airport link started late, and the proposed London – Channel Tunnel Rail Link failed to get very far at all, as political considerations forced BR to abandon its best financial route for one incorporating development objectives in the Lower Thames corridor East of London, another scheme progressed quietly. The Central Railway Group developed plans to reconstruct a through freight route between Leicester and the Channel Tunnel, largely following the Great Central alignment. This railway was planned to concentrate on the carriage of heavy goods vehicles piggy-back style, thereby extending Eurotunnel's freight shuttle into the heart of England. The Group gained themselves a Stock Exchange listing in July 1994. Was this the beginning a new railway age?

Summary

Five fat years and five lean years saw continuing improvements in the commercialisation of BR. Development in all three newly-created passenger business sectors (InterCity, Network SouthEast and Regional) improved product quality across the country. Significant railway development also occurred with 200 new stations opened. However, by the end of the decade, private sector involvement was becoming increasingly necessary in a system short of investment.

5 The Process of Privatisation

Introduction

The late 1980s saw the British Conservative Party in bold mood. Economic growth in the 1987-1989 period was very strong indeed, and large amounts of money were released into the economy by the then Chancellor, Nigel Lawson, in 1987. In the same year, the Conservatives won a general election with a huge majority of 144, and right-wing thinking was in the ascendent.

With policies which included the transfer of economic activity to the private sector, it was inevitable that the Thatcher Conservative Government of the 1980s would consider privatising the railways. Once the 'easier' targets for privatisation had successfully been floated (easy in this case meaning profit-making and organisationally simple), the more difficult industries were considered. British Rail was clearly harder on both scores – it was organisationally difficult, and it certainly required ongoing Government support.

Successive victories at the 1983 and 1987 elections enabled privatisation to progress beyond Amersham International, British Steel, British Telecom, British Gas and the regional water and electricity companies. But BR remained (with British Coal and the nuclear industry) in the 'too difficult' box. A key problem with privatising the railways was that there was no obvious method of doing so. Even non-railway staff could see that the railways were a complex industry, loss-making under current market conditions; the question was how to disentangle elements which would be attractive to the private sector. The doctrine that the private sector would inevitably provide a better service went relatively unchallenged. Underlying issues of competitive position, Government interference in nationalised industries, the costs of yet another reorganisation (including the impacts of a hiatus on the railway manufacturing sector (Ford, 1993a)), and the importance of overall economic conditions to rail traffic were only cursorily examined, and even less understood. Issues of *deregulation* and *fragmentation* (such as the loss of any economies of scale) were largely mixed up with issues of *privatisation* per se (e.g. the ability to diversify), as noted by Harris (1990). A new ownership might or might not mean a new structure for the industry.

However, confusion between these sometimes conflicting policies did not prevent privatisation of the profitable nationalised industries. That was relatively easy – but sometimes the harder part of industry deregulation came later and was dependent upon other factors (e.g. technological innovation in the telecommunications industry). The difficulties of privatising the railways were, however, recognised. Even right-winger Nicholas Ridley, one-time Secretary of State for Transport, advised the Prime Minister that BR might be 'a privatisation too far'. However, emboldened by their continuing electoral success, right-wing think tanks provided the first papers on the possibility of privatising the railways, and the debate had begun.

The debate was conducted largely through think-tank papers, and conferences (e.g. Redwood, 1988). The players in the debate were a curious mixture. Although against privatisation in principle, the trade unions and Labour Party were fairly quiet on the issue at this stage. Their view surfaced, if anywhere, indirectly in publications such as those of pressure groups (e.g. Joseph, 1989; RDS, 1989), but perhaps the most cogently-argued alternative to privatisation was the regional government model advanced by Salveson (CLES, 1989). The voice of railway managers was hardly to be heard; perhaps the political appointment of directors to the BR Board did indeed prevent genuine dialogue. On only one benefit did many agree: that separation from Government would free the railways from borrowing restrictions imposed by the Treasury (see also Harris, 1987).

Proposals for Change

A considerable group of the population clearly had fond memories of regionally-run steam railway services from between the wars (even if economic history suggested that this had not, in fact, been a successful period for the railways). These rose-tinted memories developed into a *regionally-based* solution to privatisation.

A *route-based* solution was put forward by Andrew Gritten (1988), understanding that geography alone was not an appropriate method of disaggregation. He suggested that the pre-Grouping situation (i.e. of before 1923) was a better structure to fall back upon, partly because it included more opportunities for competition.

Kenneth Irvine (1987), in a publication sponsored by the Adam Smith Insitute, however, propounded the *infrastructure authority* concept, with different operators competing to run trains on this infrastructure. Such an authority would embrace track, power supplies, signalling, stations and non-operational land. The main disadvantages of this system, however, were seen to be the difficulties in allocating costs to operators, and the monopolistic nature of the infrastructure authority which would remain distant from the real customers – passengers and freight train consignors.

However, others took the idea further, and considered mechanisms in which *slots or trainpaths* could be sold to different operators (Starkie, 1993). Slots would need to be grouped, perhaps by rolling stock diagram, so that individual trainsets could be used efficiently. This approach was unique in enabling genuine on-line competition, which otherwise was seen as needing to be postponed, in order to establish a degree of certainty, and to enable the private sector to be attracted by reducing the initial risks.

BR management were busy completing their 'Organising for Quality' programme, and it became understood that their preference was in selling off the railways *all in one piece* (recognising that privatisation in one form or another was moreoreless inevitable).

Some commentators suggested that selling off the railways by *sector* might be appropriate; this maintained the benefits of OfQ whilst still permitting privatisation to occur. Sectorisation had indeed brought the competitive market and the engineering-led railway much nearer together, and it had become a business, rather than a social service. Service groups were generally targetted at particular markets, but there were limited possibilities for competition between services; the real enemies for rail managers were the private car, the bus, the coach (deregulated coaches made some inroads into particular rail markets during the 1980s) and occasionally internal air flights.

All methods, however, acknowledged that continuing support of socially-necessary services would be necessary, although privatisation was hoped to reduce such a burden. Politically, especially with the recent defeat of the attempt to close the Settle-Carlisle line fresh in the memory, further closures were not really on the agenda. More subtly, all methods failed to address the changing nature of markets over time, and some fossilisation of the network seemed inevitable, in contrast to continuing progress in schemes such as the development of Sprinter Express, and Thameslink, services.

Why Privatise at All?

The arguments put forward above were largely political. What were the economic arguments for privatisation?

First, privatised companies are said to be more productively efficient, although analysis suggests that company size may be as important as company ownership in determining efficiency. In addition, BR had already progressed to being one of the most efficient state-owned railways in the world. However, there remained potential for further improvement. For instance, limited market testing on larger projects indicated a significant scope for *savings on the civil engineering side*; senior managers indicated that perhaps 25% of such costs could be removed. With civil engineering clearly being an important element of the budget on a railway, this is indeed significant. At the time, of course, full evidence was not available to support this contention about efficiency. However, increasing world-wide attention to the issue of railway ownership did generate interesting research. Mizutani (1994) did manage to demonstrate greater efficiency in the private, as opposed to the public, urban railways of Japan, with improved management focus suggested as a key explanation.

Secondly, the Conservative Government's view about public sector efficiency was largely self-sustaining. Governments (of all hues) had interfered with the running of the railways, chiefly through the financing mechanism. The annual Treasury spending round does not make for good investment planning, so necessary in an industry such as the railways. Further, sometimes good projects (i.e. those which met the official criteria of being financially positive, or exceeding a particular Benefit:Cost passmark for socially-necessary services) were not funded at all, leaving the railway with a legacy of higher operating costs in the future. *Access to greater funds* was clearly going to be a benefit; even though, as Conservative politicians repeatedly pointed out, the Government was the cheapest source of finance, in some cases it was simply not able to provide the cash at all.

Thirdly, private-sector companies are said to encourage better pricing of goods or services, with benefits to society accruing from a more accurate reflection of the real costs of goods. However, with rail fares being a highly-political issue, continuing regulation of them seemed inevitable. Fourthly, Governments might reasonably wish to concentrate their resources on those areas more appropriate for state provision – but is not a national rail service one of them? Fifthly, privatisation might spread share ownership and therefore help spread wealth within the population, although this 'trickle-down' hypothesis is now being challenged, as the distribution of income in society has become more skewed in recent years. Lastly, removal of the railways' monopoly was seen as essential by some, in order to increase customer focus through competition – but with an overall mode share of only 6% and considerable existing competition from the road sector, this argument is dubious.

Swedish Experience and EC Directives

A further strand of thought came from Europe. In 1988, the Swedish railway system was split into two. Swedish Railways (SJ) remained responsible for train operations, but a new company (Banverket) was established to maintain and operate the fixed infrastructure. This split of responsibilities was to be a foretaste of British experience. However, whereas in Sweden, economic theory was used to show that subsidy would be required for the infrastructure operator, in order to provide equal marginal costs to road hauliers and car drivers alike (Nilsson, 1992), the British government did not take this argument on board. Instead, they took to heart the

The Process of Privatisation

Swedish experience: SJ3 138 at Helsingborg CentralStation, on Banverket tracks [J W E Rodley]

entrepreneurial spirit of BK-Tag, a local operator in the South of Sweden who won a tender to operate local rail services for local authorities, largely through a combination of staff reductions and multi-skilling (White, 1993). This sounded more like the privatisation that British government ministers had in mind.

A split of infrastructure from operations, of course, does have some advantages, for example in management focus. With suspected support from Britain, it became enshrined in an important EC directive of 1991: 91/440. However, this directive did *not* say that infrastructure and operations had to be separately managed but merely that they had to be *separately accounted for*. This is not the same. It would have been perfectly possible for a corporate British Rail to have accounted for infrastructure separately, or for individual sectors to have done so after the completion of Organising for Quality. Instead, the British experience was to frame legislation which actually separated infrastructure from operations in a legal sense, with the creation of Railtrack.

Parliamentary Progress

A White Paper setting out the Government's proposals for maximising private sector involvement in the railways was published in July 1992 (Department of Transport, 1992a). The proposed method was largely derived from the infrastructure authority model propounded by the Adam Smith Institute, and already under development in Sweden. After consultation on the detailed operation of the franchise mechanism (DoT, 1992b), the Bill to privatise the railways was presented to Parliament in 1992, and passed in November 1993. It covered 154 sections, and made provision for:

- the establishment of a track authority to own and be responsible for the maintenance and renewal of the track and associated infrastructure, signalling, stations and depots, to control day-to-day operations of the signalling system, and to administer the timetable;
- the sale of the rail freight and parcels businesses to the private sector;
- the franchising of passenger services, with an invitation to the private sector to compete for the right to operate them;
- the establishment of a franchising authority, to negotiate, award and monitor the franchises; and
- a regulatory body to oversee track access and charging, promote competition and prevent abuse of monopoly power, to promote consumer interests and maintain network benefits.

A useful summary of the Act can be found in Glover (1996), pp. 16-20, whilst an overview document was provided by the Department of Transport (1994). The public explanation of the ideas underlying the Act continued well after this, however, including Foster's economic analysis (CRI, 1994), which had clearly influenced Government thinking. It became apparent that a key influence on proposals was a perceived requirement for the new system to provide subsidies on a much more transparent basis than had previously occurred.

With a small Government majority, individual Conservative MPs could command some political power, and the Railways Bill provided some opportunities for this. Sir Keith Speed, the MP for Ashford, had already threatened (with others) to rebel over the Channel Tunnel Rail Link Bill. Another focus of dissent was Robert Adley, the MP for Christchurch, widely respected for his understanding of the railways, and who had chaired the Select Committee examining the Bill, but who sadly died shortly afterwards. In the end, Government concessions on issues such as capping fares, avoiding network closures, and continuing the inter-availability of tickets between operators ensured that the Bill became law as the 1993 Railways Act. In fact, the Bill emerged from Parliament relatively unscathed. Pressure from the Labour Party and trade unions (who had joined with other consumer and pressure groups to form an alliance called "Save Our Railways"), led to to a certain degree of scaremongering (e.g. regarding possible service cuts, line closures, and reductions in safety), but none of the arguments really stuck. In fact, some of the key modifications were made in order to ensure the saleability of franchises (and hence the political success of the privatisation programme); for instance, a reduction in the level of inter-operator competition was enforced in the early years for this purpose (see, for instance, ORR, 1994). With some minor amendments, then, the 1992 Railways Bill became the 1993 Railways Act.

Progress in Restructuring

Although the end-point of the privatisation programme was the transfer of rail operations to the private sector (through outright sale, or the allocation of franchises for passenger services), a number of important steps had to precede this. The first stage comprised the setting-up of two key Government bodies – OPRAF and ORR – as well as the hiving-off of infrastrucutre to the new Railtrack organisation. The ongoing functions of both OPRAF and ORR are set out in chapter 6, but their initial work deserves some attention here.

The Office of the Rail Regulator (ORR) was, from the start, a legal operation based in classic legal London at Holborn. John

Swift QC was appointed as the first Rail Regulator; as he was an expert in competition law and a rail commuter from Didcot, he had as good credentials as anyone. His counterpart at the Office of Passenger Rail Franchising (OPRAF) was Roger Salmon, who set up shop in small offices in Westminster. Between them, they and their staff – appointed from a range of lawyers, civil servants, secondees from the railway industry and entirely fresh blood – spent much time agreeing the details with the Department of Transport. It is all very well Parliament passing a Bill enabling rail operators to pay charges to an infrastructure authority, but a complete charging system also had to be developed, preferably without any unduly undesirable side-effects.

The exact nature of track access agreements, and the financial regime associated with them, caused some discussion during the privatisation process, especially given the long-standing problems in attributing the joint costs of railway operation to any particular train. More transparent and train-dependent methods were recommended by a number of authors (e.g. the toll method suggested by Box (1994) or the track damage approach suggested by Harris (1992)), but the method finally chosen is dominated by a high fixed cost element (see section 6).

Public consultation was carried out by the Regulator and others in attempting to define a good regulatory framework. Proposals for the charging mechanism, for instance, had to consider what rate of return was appropriate for a monopoly provider of railway infrastructure, since no-one expected another company to set up a duplicate network. But calculating a rate of return necessitates calculating the values of the assets on which the return is to be based – and this too was the subject of debate, with estimates ranging between £1.5bn and £6bn. Some of Railtrack's potential assets, it was argued, were in such poor state of repair, that they represented a net liability. The exact value of assets was also eagerly scrutinised by the City, since it was the intention to sell Railtrack off in a trade sale, a process which occurred in May 1996, when £1.8bn was raised.

Prior to its sale, however, the City was also worried by the rate of return stipulated by the Treasury for Railtrack. This was an important issue, given the approaches being made to City institutions by potential operators. A target rate of 8% was seen as too high (Financial Times, 18th February 1994), even if this was delayed until after an initial four-year period with rates rising from 5.6%. Subsequently, however, these high rates became a bonus as investors considered the potential of Railtrack itself. These issues highlighted the inherent conflict in the roles of the Regulator, which are considered further in chapter 6.

The Regulator also held sway in determining key elements of fares policy. To avoid franchisees increasing profit simply by raising fares, Saver and Ordinary Single and Return fares were linked to the inflation rate with an RPI formula; other fares would, however, be permitted to be changed as market conditions dictated. Many of the Railcard schemes were also protected, as was the general inter-availability of ticketing between operators, but problems did occur with the latter. During 1995, the Regulator capped fares to RPI-1% for five years, thereby tilting the pendulum slightly in favour of passengers, after a number of years of above-inflation increases.

The Office of Passenger RAil Franchising (OPRAF) was set up to sell off the various passenger franchises, but initial work centred on issues such as revenue apportionment. Roger Salmon was the first Franchising Director, and led the process until Autumn 1996, by which time most of the network had been franchised. However, it was the pace of progress which attracted political comment. With another General Election due by May 1997, the Conservative Government issued directions that OPRAF should have franchised half the network by April 1996. This was an impossible deadline which was not, in fact, met. Various slippages to the privatisation programme occurred as OPRAF and the Department of Transport struggled with the administrative difficulties which politicians do not deal with, but subsequent progress caught up some of the backlog. It is expected that all franchises will indeed have been let by 31st March 1997.

A large number of consultants were appointed by the Department of Transport, OPRAF and ORR to assist in the restructuring of the industry and in sorting out the new financial arrangements. These cost significant sums of money, which are included in the analysis in chapter 7; some of the key companies are set out in Table 5.1.

Company	Area of Assistance
Linklaters & Paines	Legal
Samuel Montagu & Co	Merchant Banking
KPMG Peat Marwick	Accountancy
Coopers & Pybrand	Access Charges
Richard Ellis	Property
Dewe Rogerson	Marketing
PJR	Management & Organisation
Mercer	Freight Restructuring
Ernst & Young	Information Systems
Hambros Bank	Rolling Stock; WCML
Hill Samuel	Financing of CTRL
A D Little	Railway Research Function

Table 5.1 Consultants Appointed as part of the Rail Privatisation Programme

Before sales of individual franchises could begin, however, the industry had to be restructured. Most importantly, initial attention was focussed on the split of Railtrack (the infrastructure provider) from British Rail (the operator). Very considerable effort was put into this process, and Railtrack became a separate company (Railtrack plc) on 1 April 1994. It organised itself into ten zones, of which two were line-of-route (East Coast and West Coast main lines), whilst the rest were geographically organised. In 1995, however, to reduce overheads, the two line-of-route zones were absorbed into other zones, reducing the overall number of zones to eight. With the subsequent merger of the Southern and South-West zones, this soon became seven (see Figure 5.1).

Arrangements were also put in hand to pass over the rolling stock assets of BR to three leasing companies – Angel Trains, Eversholt Leasing and Porterbrook. There was considerable discussion in the informed press (e.g. Andred & Ford, 1993) as to how this might be done, whilst the American consultancy GATX advised the Government. In the end, the rolling stock fleet was split roughly equally between the three companies, to encourage competition. This was further encouraged by splitting up sub-fleets between them; for instance, all three had for lease 750v EMUs required for the ex-Southern region. Such a solution contrasted with the niche

The Process of Privatisation

Figure 5.1 Railtrack Zones

marketing approach suggested by Andred and Ford, who argued that an alternative approach would have been to split rolling stock into new, mid-life and heritage fleets, each of which has its uses, albeit from a different perspective. Competition between different ages of stock would, in that case, have meant competition between different companies and approaches to rolling stock provision. Reality, however, was different:

Company	Electric Locomotives	Diesel Locomotives & power cars	Electric Multiple unit vehicles	Diesel Multiple Unit vehicles
Angel	0	115	1995	1046
Eversholt	84	0	2465	0
Porterbrook	63	113	1593	734

Table 5.2 Distribution of Passenger Rolling Stock between the ROSCOs, April 1995.

The leasing charge regime was based the important principle of *'indifference pricing'*. Prices were adjusted for the earning potential

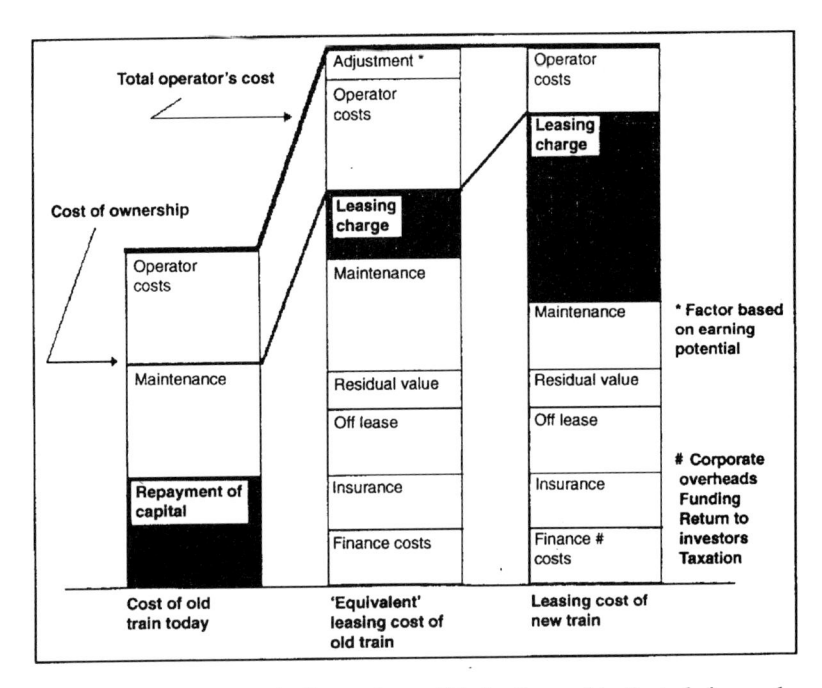

Figure 5.2 Diagrammatic Comparison of Train Ownership Costs before and after Privatisation

(Source: Modern Railways, December 1993)

of the rolling stock, so that older trains (with their higher maintenance requirements) were cheaper than more modern stock. Overall, this left potential service providers with a finely-balanced choice, as the total cost to them of the different rolling stock types was broadly equal (see Fig. 5.2). However, as can be seen, the total cost of using rolling stock did increase with privatisation. As this was in addition to other cost increases which occurred at the time, the real cost of purchasing rolling stock doubled from £400,000 to around £800,000 per vehicle between 1990 and 1995.

The costs of leasing rolling stock were (and remain) relatively high. The magazine Modern Railways reported in March 1994 that annual lease charges for two-car diesel multiple units ranged from £80,000 for 'Pacer' railbuses to £200,000 for Class 158 Express Sprinter units. For mainline locomotives such as the Class 47, figures of up to £400,000 were mentioned. The importance of these high figures is three-fold: first, it ensures that the ROSCOs are extremely profitable; secondly, it reduces the proportion of costs controllable by TOCs; thirdly, it increases the net subsidy required from Central Government.

The profitability of the ROSCOs soon attracted attention from other companies. By early 1997, Porterbrook's management had sold out to Stagecoach, and Eversholt's to HSBC. In both cases, the companies were valued at over £200m more than they had originally been sold for (Porterbrook, originally sold for £527m, was re-sold for £825m, whilst Eversholt went from £580 to £726m). This led to individual managers becoming millionaires overnight, and to accusations that the original sale price had been too low.

Vesting and PSRs

Before rail passenger franchises could be let, BR passenger operations needed to be split into service groups which would form the basis for the franchises. 25 Train Operating Units (TOUs) were formed within British Rail, very closely mirroring the existing sub-sectors; notable changes included the creation of new TOUs for the urban networks of Liverpool and Cardiff, as the Merseyrail and Cardiff TOUs. However, this process was more important in accounting terms than practically – although passengers writing cheques did notice that they were asked to make them payable to the TOU, not to BR itself. A legal change was then brought about, in order to make TOUs into TOCs – or Train Operating Companies. These were genuine subsidiary companies of the BRB, and this process – of vesting – took place gradually throughout 1995.

In addition to vesting, it was also necessary to define what level of service would be tendered for, and OPRAF set itself the task of defining the minimum level of service for every route in the country. There was widespread confusion – fuelled by the Save Our Railways group and others – about the role of the Passenger Service Requirements (PSRs). These were not timetable specifications – which was just as well, given that the minimum level of service specified was broadly 90% for rural and urban services, but only around 60% for InterCity TOCs. In order that every minor timetable change in the future did not require reference to OPRAF, the PSRs set out a basic minimium which was required – in such terms as journey time, frequency, and first and last departure times. If franchisees operate a poorer service than that specified in the PSR, then OPRAF reserve the right to withhold grant, and/or the ORR to intervene. Although punctuality, cancellations and station booking office opening hours are monitored, notable exceptions within PSRs are attributes of journey quality – only with the Merseyrail franchise did documents begin to refer to litter-picking, graffitti removal or refreshment facilities.

But where does operational flexibility become a charter for closure? OPRAF argued that commercial judgment was best to determine the exact level of service, although they never acknowledged that sometimes the private sector makes mistakes as well as the much-maligned nationalised industries. Higher service levels were to be enforceable in the less profitable TOCs, for reasons of social benefit. No-one, however, answered the question as to how the Franchising Director would cope with a reduced grant from the Treasury.

Once vesting of a company had occurred, and the PSR had been agreed, it was then possible for the final stage of privatisation to go ahead. As it was clearly never going to be possible to franchise all 25 TOCs overnight (nor even together, given the complexity of operation), OPRAF decided to group the TOCs. Those franchises with complicating elements such as involvement with PTEs (e.g. Regional Railways North East), or dependent upon major Government-supported infrastructure schemes (such as Thameslink) were deferred to the end of the line.

The process of franchising began with a pre-qualification stage (OPRAF, 1994), followed by a formal invitation to tender for a particular franchise. After indicative bids had been received, a short-listing process occurred, usually with four bidders remaining. One of these was subsequently named as the preferred bidder, and was given around a fortnight to complete financing and other organisational arrangements before being confirmed as franchise winner. At that point, OPRAF gave details of the bid, in terms of the subsidy required, and the service improvements promised.

The three franchises selected for the first batch were South West Trains, the London Tilbury & Southend line, and Great West trains. Political considerations certainly played a part in this selection. SWT serves a considerable proportion of the London business community, in its commuting journeys, whilst LT&S had

The Process of Privatisation

already been dubbed 'the Misery line', through a combination of old rolling stock and ancient signalling. Replacement signalling was authorised in 1992, coming on stream just in time to coincide with operation in the private sector.

Franchising Progress

Whilst administrative arrangements were being made, potential bidders were also beginning to emerge. The Government claimed that around 150 private sector companies were seriously interested, but it is thought that these included a number of banks who registered for information in order to assist clients. Richard Tomkins, writing in the Financial Times of 21st July 1993, identified only 16 genuine potential bidders. The list below is interesting, in enabling a comparison with the actual position which emerged subsequently.

Company	Comments
Badger Rail*	Became part of First Bus group
British Airways	
British Bus	Bidding with MBO team for Thameslink
Burlington Northern	
Canadian Pacific	
EYMS Group*	Management involved in formation of Prism Rail
Go-Ahead Northern*	Assisted MBO team for Thames Trains
Grampian Regional Transport*	Became part of First Bus group
MTL Trust Holdings*	
National Express*	
Rider Group*	Became part of First Bus group
Sea Containers*	
Southern Vectis	Unsuccessful bid for Island line
Stagecoach Rail*	
West Midlands Travel*	Became part of National Express Group
Virgin Group*	

Table 5.3 Potential Franchise Bidders Identified in 1993
Those asterisked were successful bidders

OPRAF grouped franchises into batches, and all went through a similar process of Invitation to Pre-Qualify, ITT (Invitation To Tender), short-listing and eventual selection. The timetable for this process, once established, covered around nine months, although the first few took well over a year. The first batch of six was also whittled down to three.

Early research by Preston et al (1996) indicated that key issues to possible bidders were:

- costs and errors in bidding;
- the separation of infrastructure from other parts of the railway;
- less competition and a more self-contained network; and
- the length of franchises.

Bidders from outside the railway were more optimistic regarding the opportunities for cutting costs, but all could see the potential for increasing revenue. Our analysis, however, (see chapter 7) shows that different factors were critical in determining the actual price bid for franchises, as the above issues were generally concerns common to all participants.

The first franchise, SWT, was let on December 19th 1995, with private-sector rail operations due to begin on February 4th. However, the announcement was somewhat overshadowed by the discovery of a fraud on LT&S. This none-too-subtle fraud involved transfer of Travelcard tickets between Fenchurch Street (where 22% of revenue should have been passed on to London Transport) and Upminster (where 48% of revenue should have been). This fiddle – allegedly carried out by a member of staff being sent with a suitcase of tickets from Fenchurch Street to Upminster on a frequent basis – was already thought to have cost LT £45,000 in the six weeks it had been going on (an annual rate of £500,000). On a small franchise with a turnover of £25 million, such a difference of £500,000 would clearly have been significant. As a result of this, the management team, previously the preferred bidder, were disqualified, and the entire bidding process recommenced for that franchise.

In addition, problems had occurred with the Great West Trains franchise, as the preferred bidders (Resurgence Railways, led by an ex-BR manager, although not an MBO in the normal sense) were unable to raise the financial support required by OPRAF in the fortnight allowed, and the franchise was passed to the second bidder, G W Holdings (a MEBO supported by a late contribution from FirstBus). Although these issues provided some political ammunition for detractors of privatisation, the process was not derailed.

The Process of Privatisation

Monday 4th February 1996 saw the first privatised trains running on the British rail network in nearly 50 years. Few people turned out for the first train in the London area (the 0510 Twickenham – Waterloo), although Sir George Young, MP for Acton, and Transport Secretary at the time, was amongst them. Less charitable were the observations that the first train which should have run, GWT's 0150 Fishguard – Paddington, actually ran as a substitute bus, due to engineering works.

A further interesting development was the challenge in the High Court by the "Save Our Railways" group, declaring that aspects of the minimum Passenger Service Requirement were illegal. Although the Court ruled that some amendments would be required to franchises not yet let, this did not apply retrospectively, and the franchises already in operation continued unhindered.

The remainder of 1996 saw continuing progress with franchising, with companies beginning private sector operations whilst others, behind them in the process, were let (see Table 5.4). Although there was some question as to the real level of interest from genuine buyers, a reasonable range of companies were indeed involved in the process eventually. Bus companies featured strongly, with Stagecoach, winners of the first franchise (SWT), publicly committing themselves to bidding for all 25 franchises. In retrospect, however, their prices have been uncompetitive.

Minimising subsidy payments appeared to drive OPRAF's choice for bidders, especially at first. Smaller bidders were generally less successful, which was attributed to difficulties in raising and sustaining finance. Certainly, management buy-outs (MBOs) were unsuccessful until they joined forces with outside parties, such as the Chiltern/Laing (M40) bid for services out of Marylebone.

The pace of letting franchises picked up, as OPRAF climbed the learning curve, and were set targets of completing the programme by 31st March 1997. However, the Labour Party, who were wondering how to deal with the railways when they came to power, accused the Government of a 'scorched-earth' policy, deliberately designed to make things difficult.

	SWT	GWT	ICEC	GEx	MML	NSC	LTS	Chilt	SE	SW&W	CV	Thames	Island
began operation	04/02/96	04/02/96	28/04/96	28/04/96	28/04/96	26/05/96	26/05/96	21/07/96	15/06/96	13/10/96	13/10/96	13/10/96	13/10/96
National Express		S	S	W	W	S		S	S		S		W
Stagecoach	W	S	S			B	S	S	S	W	W	S	
Prism				S	S		W			W			
FirstBus		B							B				
MTL Trust Holdings					S					S			
Go-Ahead Group												B	
Connex (CGEA)	B		B			W		S	W				
Sea Containers	S		W										
Virgin				S									
Resurgence Railways		P										S	
G B Railways							S		S				
Man Buy-Outs	S	W		S	S	S	P	W	S	S	S	W	
Great Western Holdings										S			
Halcrow											S		
M40 Trains												S	
GOVIA (Go-Ahead/VIA GTI)													
British Bus													

The Process of Privatisation

	ICXC	Anglia	GE	WAGN	Mersey	NLR	Thlink	Central	NWRR	RRNE	ICWC	Scot	Short-listed	Won
began operation	05/01/97	05/01/97	05/01/97	05/01/97	02/02/97	--/02/97	--/02/97	03/03/97	03/03/97	03/03/97	03/03/97			
National Express		S				W		W				W	10	5
Stagecoach	S				S			S	S		S	S	14	2
Prism		S		W	S			S	S			S	12	4
FirstBus		S	W	B			B	B					6	1
MTL Trust Holdings					W		S	S		W			5	2
Go-Ahead Group					S								2	1
Connex (CGEA)			B			S		S	S				9	2
Sea Containers											S		4	1
Virgin	W			S			S				W		6	2
Resurgence Railways		W											1	0
G B Railways				S			S						5	1
Man Buy-Outs			S	S			S	P		S		S	18	3
Great Western Holdings	S					S							4	1
Halcrow								W					1	0
M40 Trains													1	0
GOVIA (Go-Ahead/VIA GTI)							W			B		S	3	1
British Bus							B						1	1

Table 5.4 Analysis of Key Franchise Bidders
(adapted, with permission, from Rail Privatisation News)

B = financial backer for MBO bid   P = preferred bidder   S = shortlisted bidder   W = franchise winner

79

A matrix of franchise bidders is set out in Table 5.4. It was suggested that, as maters progressed, a considerable number of different companies were deliberately awarded franchises (perhaps in order to minimise the risk of monopolies subsequently developing as they have in the British bus industry); nevertheless, National Express landed up with five franchises.

Sales of Other Companies

The franchising process was not the only way in which constituents of the erstwhile BR passed out of existence. The freight businesses were all sold off. Despite management consultancy advice to the contrary, the three trainload businesses (Mainline, Loadhaul and Transrail) were eventually all sold together to the US-based Wisconsin Central railroad for £225m on the 24th February 1996. Wisconsin who also acquired the Res parcels business. The pro-rail positive reputation of Wisconsin's President Ed Burkhardt allayed fears about a sale to a foreign buyer, although accidents on a number of systems with which Wisconsin had an involvement (including a fatal accident at Stafford on the 9th March) did not get their public relations off to a good start.

Some of the freight companies were more difficult to sell, with more than one attempt being needed at Freightliner, eventually sold to its management. Railfreight Distribution also proved a problem, although its alleged financial performance (£70m p.a. loss on £70m p.a. turnover) made it less attractive to the private sector. Vested in October 1996, it nevertheless attracted bids from Freightliner's new management, EW&S, Transfesa, National Power, GE Capital (from the USA) and logistics company Tibbett & Britten. Unsurprisingly, EW&S were successful, no doubt with a strategy of growth also designed to share costs with its other freight operations, particularly the 'Enterprise' wagonload network.

A continuing programme of sales of other minor companies also continued, including the Infrastructure Maintenance Units (IMUs) and Track Renewal Units (TRUs), design and consultancy offices, quarries and permanent way works; a full list is given in Appendix 1. Some companies were closed down, if none of the offers for them were deemed to be acceptable.

Analysis with Hindsight

The initial debate about methods of privatisation was largely based on political argument, rather than fact. A number of interesting alternatives were provided as potential models for the industry, without much supporting analysis being able to indicate the likely costs and benefits. Research and understanding of railway privatisation issues clearly developed during the process, and a particularly interesting study was carried out by the Institute for Transport Studies at the University of Leeds, sponsored by the Economic and Social Research Council. Using analytical techniques from the field of economics, they continued their previous work on comparing railways across Europe (where the differing systems in Sweden and the Netherlands out-perform the others), and were able to estimate the optimum size for a railway system.

Management theory suggests that any industry will have economies of scale, in which savings can indeed be made as joint overheads are shared. Industries also have diseconomies of scale, where increasing size brings poorer performance as issues of multiple objectives, geographical dispersion, and a distancing from workers, become important. Preston (1993) showed that, on the basis of European railway experience, a split of BR's passenger business into three would have most probably provided the best economic solution. This suggests that, economically at least, the sector-based solution could have been the best; it also confirms that the solution actually chosen was much too complicated.

Summary

A range of alternative methods of privatisation were considered, even if all were based on the unsupported assertion that the private sector would inevitably provide a better service. EC directive 91/440 was used to support a separation of infrastructure from operations; passenger services were to be franchised. Proposals were enacted in 1993, and progress was made in industry restructuring, the set-up of OPRAF and ORR as new Government bodies, and the establishment of new contractual relationships. Passenger franchises were let throughout 1996, during which year many other subsidiary companies were sold outright.

6 The New Structure

As we have seen, the 'privatisation' of British Rail actually entailed two, quite separate, elements. First came the restructuring of the industry; only then was it possible to sell or franchise various parts of it. This chapter summarises the post-privatisation structure of mainline railways in Britain.

The Old Structure

After nationalisation in 1948, British Rail provided a whole range of railway-related services. Some of these (e.g. hotels and Sealink shipping services) had been sold off well before any consideration of the privatisation of the railway operating businesses, but even in the late 1980s, BR retained control over a vast range of activities. With the Sector-led railway, Sector directors did indeed control most elements of their railway, including such disparate elements as track maintenance gangs, train drivers, catering staff, signal design engineers and ticket inspectors.

As we have seen in earlier chapters, British Rail was subject to a large number of external pressures, the response to some of which had been changes in organisational structure. However, from 1979 onwards, although reorganisation was effectively carried out on a continuous basis, productivity continued to improve. Cochrane (1992) showed how the engineering-led organisation had been replaced by a matrix structure, with both regional and functional managers having authority. This system was replaced by the 'Organising for Quality' (OfQ) initiative, which was implemented in 1993. Against this background, yet another structure was developed as part of the privatisation and fragmentation of the industry.

The New Structure

A key element of the restructuring of the industry was the separation of infrastructure-related tasks from operating tasks. As a result,

The New Structure

civil, power and signalling engineering tasks passed to Railtrack, as infrastructure owner; Railtrack's operating staff covered the key role of signalling and control. However, Railtrack does not itself carry out engineering tasks with its own staff, but instead subcontracts these to specialist engineering contractors. This was identified early on as a potential saving, since internal railway engineering costs were known to be more expensive than could be procured elsewhere.

All passenger and freight train services are already in the hands of private companies, with previous passenger operations having been franchised, and freight operations sold off. New (private) operators may also compete with the existing operators, although after a delay on the passenger side. The vast majority of rolling stock is, however, not owned by operators but by leasing companies, although both Railtrack and (particularly the freight) train operators also own some stock.

In summary, companies in the new industry fall into the following main categories:

- Infrastructure Owner – Railtrack (split into seven geographically-based zones)
- Franchised Passenger Operators – the 25 Train Operating Companies (TOCs)
- Unregulated Passenger Operators e.g. EPS (operators of Eurostar international trains)
- Open Access Operators (operating without a franchise) e.g. Heathrow Express
- Non-Passenger Operators e.g. EW&S (freight) Railways, Freightliner
- The three Rolling Stock Leasing Companies (LEASCOs or ROSCOs) (Angel Trains, Eversholt & Porterbrook)
- Contractors (Infrastructure Maintenance Units (IMUs) and Track Renewal Units (TRUs), which became companies (IMCs and TRCs) prior to their individual sale)
- The (Passenger) Franchising Director – Office of Passenger Rail Franchising (OPRAF)
- The Regulator – Office of the Rail Regulator (ORR)

- The Safety Regulator – Her Majesty's Railway Inspectorate (HMRI) as part of the Health & Safety Executive (HSE)
- Local Authorities (in the metropolitan areas, via the Passenger Transport Executives (PTEs))
- Other suppliers of goods and services e.g. Adtranz (rolling stock), Westinghouse (signals), DCA (design), many others with specialisms ranging from architects to project managers to cleaners. Note that some of these are ex-BR units, whilst others have much longer histories in the private sector, and yet others have been recently set up, sensing a market opportunity in the new environment.

Figure 6.1 gives a summary of the industry structure. Further comments on many of the individual organisations are given below.

Miles of track	20000
Route miles of track	10000
Leased Stations	2500
Operated Major Stations	14
Miles of Sea Defences	124
Bridges, Viaducts and Tunnels	40000
Level Crossings	9000
Signalling Staff & Supervisors	6000
Other Employees	5500

Table 6.1 Statistical Summary of Railtrack plc

Railtrack

Railtrack was created by the 1993 Railways Act, and began trading in April 1994. Its key purpose is to own, maintain and develop Britain's mainline rail infrastructure. Its large size can be understood by realising that it immediately became one of the country's largest 100 companies (and hence represented on the FTSE-100), when successfully sold off in 1996. Key facts about the size of its operation are set out in Table 6.1.

Financial Performance

Railtrack's financial performance requires careful consideration. Its income is derived by charging rail service operators fees for

The New Structure

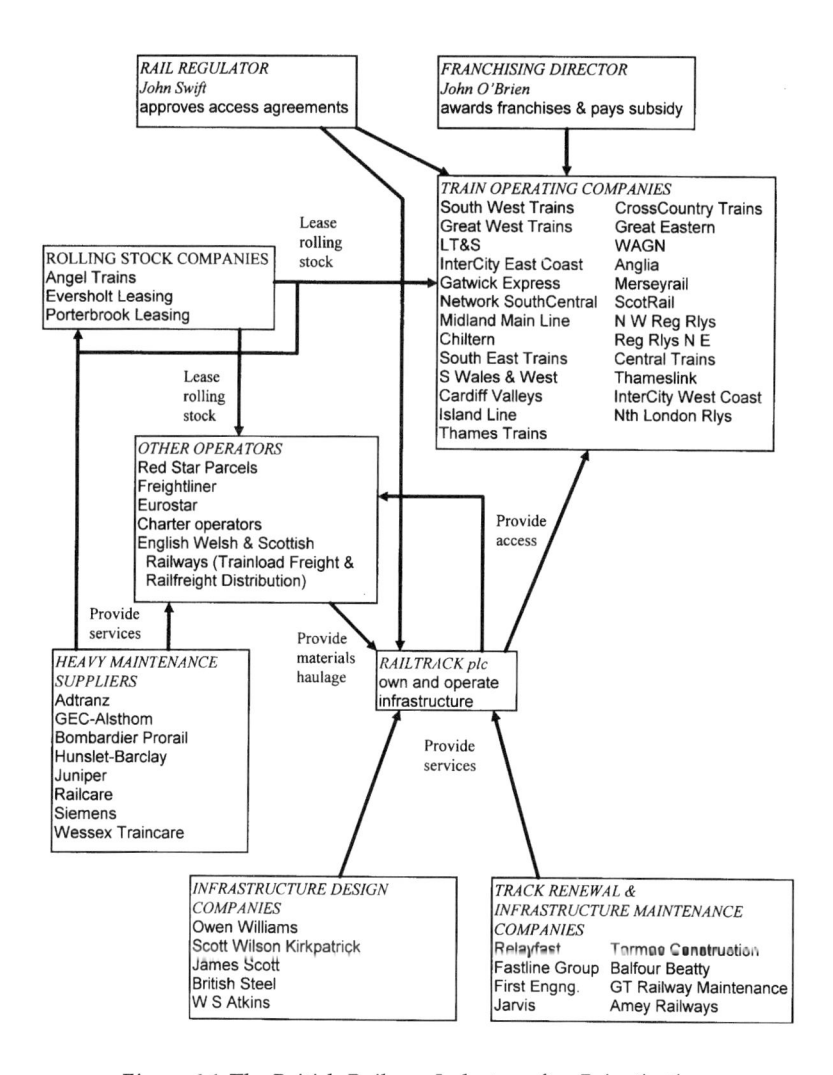

Figure 6.1 The British Railway Industry after Privatisation

using its tracks. However, as a monopoly, the prices which it can charge for access to its network are regulated by the Rail Regulator. As with other regulated industries (e.g. water, electricity), the Regulator can have a very significant impact upon the financial performance of a company.

Track maintenance workers such as these work on Railtrack infrastructure but are employed by Infrastructure Maintenance Companies (IMCs). [E.W. Godward]

In 1995/6, Railtrack realised profits of around £300m on a turnover of £2300m, its income predominantly coming from track access charges paid by TOCs, and underwritten by the Franchising Director. (It should be remembered that Britain's railways are effectively passenger railways; around 90% of Railtrack's income is from passenger operators). Some of Railtrack's profit, however, has come from an acknowledged under-investment in its infrastructure, as recognised in its Network Management Statements (see below). Asset management plans have taken longer than anticipated to develop, and late in 1996 the Regulator issued an official warning about the increasing backlog of investment, then running at £333m. Table 6.2 sets out an indicative preliminary assessment of Railtrack. The percentage change columns highlight the fact that, although revenues have increased, so have costs. Railtrack have stated that this is to clear the backlog of work which had built up both during BR ownership, and in Railtrack's period of state ownership. It will be interesting to watch how the company develops its plans over the next few years.

The New Structure

	1994-5 total £m	1995-6 1st half £m	1995-6 2nd half £m	1995-6 total £m	1996-7 1st half £m	% change 1st half 96-7 on 95-6	% change full year 95-6 on 94-5
Income							
Passenger Franchise Revenue	1955	1001	1002	2003	1046	+4.4	+2.5
Freight Revenue	191	72	86	158	79	+9.7	-17.3
Property Income	82	56	56	112	58	+3.5	+36.6
Other Income	47	10	17	27	21	+110.0	-42.6
Total Income	2275	1139	1161	2300	1204	+5.7	+1.1
Costs							
Production & Management	501	239	218	457	247	+3.3	-8.8
Infrastructure Maintenance	696	348	377	725	371	+6.6	+4.0
Asset Maintenance Plan Charge	483	253	250	503	259	+2.3	+4.1
Joint Industry Costs	197	96	116	212	100	+4.1	+7.6
Depreciation	93	52	55	107	58	+11.5	+15.1
Total Costs	1970	988	1016	2004	1035	+4.8	+1.7

Table 6.2 *Railtrack plc: Financial Performance 1994-7*

Property

As well as being the provider of infrastructure Railtrack is an important owner of property. The importance of property and its development on railway finances have long been recognised in railway business history. During the privatisation of Railtrack, the prospectus (Warburg, 1996) put the value of the property assets at about £1.4 billion. Although British Rail's major land holdings had included many acres of derelict land that had formerly been sidings, yards and depots, it also possessed a great number of lucrative city centre sites. Where rationalisation and closures had occurred, some sites were sold off but more usually the leasehold only was sold, with BR as freeholder extracting rent from the site. Most importantly, BR redeveloped many of its major stations in partnership with office and retail developers. Stations such as London's Liverpool Street were extensively refurbished and redeveloped. Seven platforms were roofed over to provide a base for the Bishopsgate Office Development, which subsequently housed the likes of NatWest Capital Markets and the EBRD.

The fragmentation of the industry saw much of the property portfolio transferred to Railtrack. It now manages 14 of the larger

Railtrack asset: Liverpool Street Station. [N.G. Harris]

stations directly, including most of the London termini such as Liverpool Street. Smaller stations come under the control of one of the Train Operating Units/Companies, who lease or rent the station from Railtrack, sub-leasing to other TOCs as appropriate.

Network Management Statements and Investment in Infrastructure

Railtrack are required to produce Network Management Statements, describing the planning and future development of the railway network (Railtrack, 1995a, 1997). The first statement indicated that assessment of a sample of the assets had revealed geographical variations in maintenance and renewal practice. The immediate requirement was to develop a consistent set of policies to maintain and review the assets. The expectation was that £1 bn p.a. would be spent on such renewals and maintenance over the period 1995/6-2004-5. However, the Rail Regulator had approved access charges on the basis that £3.5bn would be spent on maintaining, renewing *and enhancing* rail infrastructure.

The New Structure

Although the statement had been drawn up in consultation with:
- operators of passenger and freight railway services
- Passenger Transport Executives and Local Authorities
- other existing or proposed rail infrastructure operators
- airport and other transport operators
- the Department of Transport
- the Director of Passenger Rail Franchising
- the Rail Regulator
- the European Commission

it was the Regulator who was to indicate dissatisfaction with the degree of funds being spent on developing the network. In December 1996 he wrote to Railtrack estimating that, over the 2.5 years since the formation of Railtrack, the degree of underspend had been £333m.

There had been an ongoing argument from the time of BR about underspending on maintenance and the renewal of assets. The case mentioned was the condition of the West Coast Main Line (WCML). Concern had been expressed since the 1970s, and projects (which would have brought about speed increases and service development) had been developed to address these concerns. However, the pressures on capital spending by BR and by Government conspired to ensure that the necessary investment did not occur.

The WCML had been modernised and electrified between 1960 and 1967 (the Southern part) and between 1970 and 1974 (between Crewe and Glasgow). This was successful in boosting patronage, with faster and more reliable services. However, as the condition of the infrastructure deteriorated, and the rolling stock was not renewed, replaced or refurbished, traffic declined in the face of road and air competition.

The proposed Railtrack route modernisation would provide more reliable train services, more frequent train services, and a modernised train control system. If train operators are willing to fund developments, then improvements could be made, such as:

- 225km/hr operation using tilting trains to reduce journey times
- gauge enlargements to accommodate piggyback, swap-body and High Cube containers

The Piggyback consortium (a grouping of 40 interested parties (including Railtrack) concerned with piggyback, swap-body and container operations) had cost estimates carried out for the proposed works. At the end of 1996, however, Railtrack's own estimates were three times higher, and complaints ensued. Railtrack's estimate of £308m for improvements between Dollands Moor (freight yard for the Channel Tunnel) and Mossend (near Glasgow) was stated by its Commercial Director Michael Howell to be both realistic and based on field studies. Estimates were also prepared for extensions to Trafford Park (Manchester), Seaforth (Liverpool) and one of the ports serving Ireland (Holyhead or Heysham). These estimates were submitted to the Department of Transport, and submissions for rail freight grants are to be made in 1997.

The WCML is also the UK's part of the European Commission's 14 priority projects to achieve a Trans European Network of key routes. In 1997, European funding of £5.75m was given for studies to develop it. The components of the WCML modernisation are:

- A new train control system (probably transmission-based), coupled to Automatic train Protection. This would give greater train capacity, and an opportunity to improve information systems;
- A single control centre, replacing a large number of signal boxes;
- Upgraded traction power systems;
- Upgraded track condition, coupled with new maintenance strategies.

The 1995 Network Management Statement also covered information on significant resignalling and infrastructure schemes. Many of these schemes had been inherited from BR. The major renewal schemes were all running late, by between one and 11 years. Clearly the latter was only partly Railtrack's fault, but nevertheless, these facts support the concerns of the Regulator.

The statement also identified 32 major renewal schemes to be completed between 1999 and 2005. These will include features to improve reliability, and will permit longer trains to operate. The statement highlights the effective rate of track renewals to be achieved, compared to what had been achieved previously. The

Fig 6.2 Railtrack plc Investment Profile (source: Railtrack 1997)

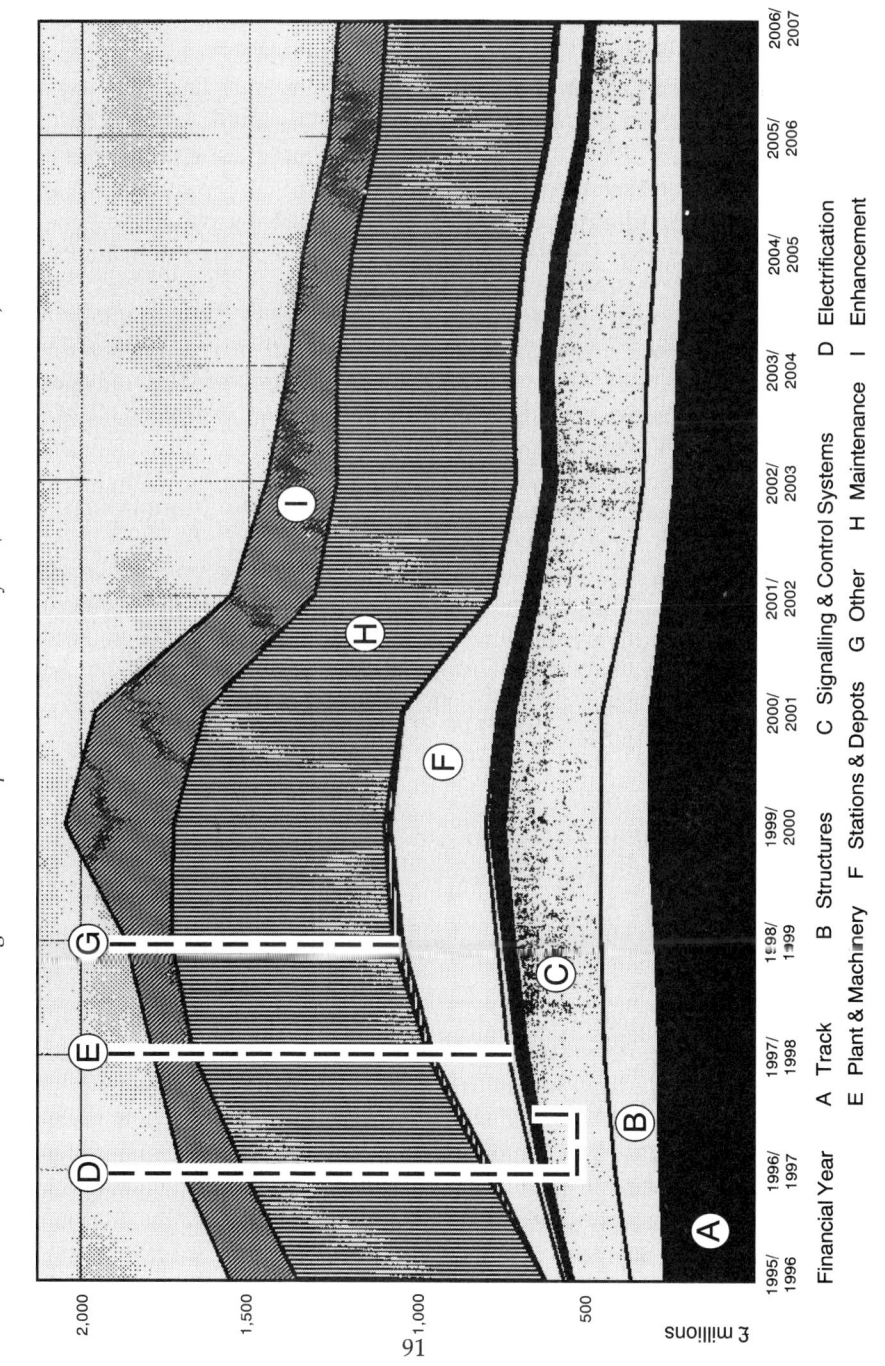

A Track   B Structures   C Signalling & Control Systems   D Electrification
E Plant & Machinery   F Stations & Depots G Other   H Maintenance   I Enhancement

statement notes: "The forecast rate of renewals is considerably higher for sleeper and ballast than over the preceding five years; the rate for rail is lower, as a result of technical allowances."

The publication of the 1997 network management statement in February set out to rebut the Regulator's criticisms of an underspend. Railtrack state, however, that they will have spent £1bn more than the Regulator expected. It will be interesting to watch how this argument develops over the coming years. The expected investment profile is shown in Figure 6.2, and shows a typical railway investment wave profile. An increasing level of investment over the next four years is then followed by a period when investment levels decline, levelling out at around £1.4bn per annum.

Figure 6.2 shows the investments to be made by Railtrack in nominal terms. However, to begin to see the real value of the investment in today's terms the investments must be discounted at an appropriate rate. For the sake of simplicity the discount rate used is 8%. Table 6.3 shows the discounted values for the three categories of investment.

Investment type	Nominal value £m - 1996/97 prices	Discounted value at 8%
Maintenance	5670	3903
Renewal	8280	5799
Enhancement	1940	1325
TOTAL	15890	11028

Table 6.3 Investment in the Railtrack Network 1997/8-2006/7
(source: Railtrack, 1997)

Summary

In its first couple of years, Railtrack performed poorly on a number of public relations issues, including dealing with a number of accidents. Problems with the acceptance process for new trains (EECSAP), and a number of derailments in the Euston and Camden areas attributed to poor track maintenance, added to the image problem, suggested by some commentators to reflect the less commercial approach of some of the ex-BR staff who had transferred to Railtrack. However, more recent performance has suggested that management are coming to grips with a number of the key issues, which is critical for the success of the industry as a whole; if Railtrack does not perform well, the new industry structure cannot.

Train Operating Companies

The Train Operating Companies were sold as franchises based on the Train Operating Units set up under the British Railways Board under the 1993 Act. Key statistics about the individual companies are set out in Table 6.4. 13 groupings of franchises have emerged, and their financial performance to date is summarised in Table 6.5. Note that management buy-outs have been successful only occasionally, and only with outside assistance.

Prism Rail plc

Prism was specifically established to tender for the rail franchises on offer, and has won four of them. The company's founders had experience in the bus industry, and floated the company on the Alternative Investment Market (AIM) on the 29th May 1996.

The first franchise of LTS (operated from the 26th May 1996) was joined by South Wales and West and Cardiff Valleys (from 13th October) and West Anglia Great Northern (WAGN) (from 5th January 1997). The interim report published on 16th December 1996 gives some indications of the financial performance, but only as they relate to LTS (see Table 6.5).

GB Railways Ltd

GB Railways was also set up to exploit the opportunities thrown up by the rail franchising process. They took control of Anglia Railways on 5th January 1997, and obtained a listing on the AIM through a share placing on the 6th. Like Prism, immediately after the listing and placing of shares at £1, they moved to a significant premium.

Stagecoach Holdings plc

Stagecoach began as a coach operator after bus deregulation in 1983, and has grown to be the third largest bus operating group in the UK. It was capitalised at £1.664bn in December 1996, and has bus operating subsidiaries in New Zealand, Malawi, Kenya, Portugal and Sweden. Prior to their forays into rail franchises, their rail experience included the provision of cheaper overnight seating on Anglo-Scottish sleeper trains in 1991 when InterCity withdrew the

	Train op costs £m	Access charges £m	Train Leases £m	Total Costs £m	Fares Revenue £m	Subsidy £m	Train Miles m	Journeys m	Pass Miles m	Ave. Jny Length miles	Average Train Load	Average Fare/Jny £
Ex-InterCity businesses												
Anglia	17	25.8	8.83	51.63	31	20.63	3.5	5.8	361	62	103	5.34
CrossCountry	61	95.7	40.15	196.85	112	84.85	9.6	10	1275	128	133	11.20
East Coast	56	155.6	42.65	254.25	217	37.25	9.7	10	1095	110	113	21.70
Gatwick Express	6	7.4	5.73	19.13	27	-7.87	1.3	3.6	95	26	73	7.50
Great Western	46	110.4	50.64	207.04	156	51.04	7.9	14	1218	87	154	11.14
Midland Mainline	20	40.5	16.7	77.2	58	19.2	3.2	5.3	437	82	137	10.94
West Coast	70	157.3	47.79	275.09	221	54.09	12	12	1909	159	159	18.42
Ex Network SouthEast businesses												
Chiltern	4	23	4.5	31.5	15	16.5	2.6	5.2	136	26	52	2.88
Great Eastern	33	61.6	45.3	139.9	108	31.9	6.4	47	897	19	140	2.30
Island Line	2.6	0	0.4	3.0	0.9	2.1	0.2	1.1	4.3	4	22	0.82
LTS Rail	14	36	17.8	67.8	53	14.8	3.1	23	423	18	136	2.30
Network South Central	57	98.5	43.6	199.1	158	41.1	13.3	83	1250	15	94	1.90
North London Railways	23	50.5	17.3	90.8	52	38.8	4.9	32	434	14	89	1.63
South Eastern	74	162.8	125.1	361.9	205	156.9	16	103	1602	16	100	1.99
South West Trains	79	154.6	55.7	289.3	221	68.3	18	95	1800	19	100	2.33
Thames	26	36	16	78	39	39	5	21	325	15	65	1.86
Thameslink	25	39.6	21.7	86.3	61	25.3	5.3	23	451	20	85	2.65
WAGN	47	115	37.4	199.4	103	96.4	10.7	47	797	17	74	2.19

Ex-Regional Railways businesses

Cardiff Railway	3.5	22	3	28.5	6.5	22	2.0	6.9	61	9	31	0.94
Central	61	123.5	23.84	208.14	70	138.14	16	29	656	23	41	2.41
Merseyrail Electrics	45	38	20	103	21	82	3.4	30	177	6	52	0.70
North East	63	146.3	31.68	240.98	62	178.98	19	34	720	21	38	1.82
North West	61	41.2	41.2	143.4	47	96.4	14.6	27	455	17	31	1.74
ScotRail	67	161	44.86	272.86	90	182.86	19.2	51	915	18	48	1.76
SW&W	40	18.2	18.2	76.4	39	37.4	10	11	422	38	42	3.55

Sources: Department of Transport, 1992b; Ford, quoted in Madgin, 1995

Table 6.4 Estimated Summary Statistics about the Train Operating Companies, 1993–4

facility. Unfortunately, this did not prove to be a financial success, and the services were withdrawn after 12 months.

Stagecoach are known to have bid for nearly all the franchises, but they only won two (South West (operated from 4th February 1996) and Island Line (from 13th October). The performance of South West Trains was reported in their Annual Report and Accounts.

At the end of July 1996, they proposed the acquisition of the rolling stock company Porterbrook. This was sanctioned after undertakings were given to the regulatory authorities concerning the leasing of trains to competitors' train operating franchisees.

Virgin

Virgin is the private company of Richard Branson, with a reputation in marketing. Although widely diversified, it has major interests in leisure and air transport. The group has an annual turnover of £1.8bn, and is split into eight autonomous divisions.

Virgin won both the InterCity Cross Country and West Coast franchises, with the stated aim of doubling traffic on each. However, these are not their only rail projects; they also have a stake in the London & Continental Railways (LCR) consortium (see below). Their winning bid for Cross Country involves the transfer of train maintenance to National Express' Midland Main Line. MML have become responsible for all maintenance, servicing, cleaning and fuelling of Cross Country's trains.

National Express Group plc

The National Express Group was privatised out of the National Bus Company, and is the major provider of interurban coach services in the UK. It took over West Midlands Travel bus company in 1995, owns East Midlands and Bournemouth airports, and had a market capitalisation of £501m in December 1996. They are also part of the LCR consortium.

From 28th April 1996, the Group operated the franchises for Gatwick Express and the Midland Main Line. The winning bid for the latter brought with it a referral to the Monopolies and Mergers Commission (MMC, 1996) because National Express already operated coach services on similar routes. In statements issued in November 1996, the chief executive, Ernie Patterson, stated that competition came "– from cars, not coaches, and that the overlap only concerns seven – some of them lossmaking – routes in the Midlands."

The main findings of the MMC study were that:
- the test of competitive supply was met from Sheffield, Chesterfield, Derby, Nottingham and Leicester; and
- the share of supply test was met from all five towns.

The Commission stated that there had, prior to the award of the franchise, been competition between rail and coach services. This had been lost when National Express had been awarded the MML franchise. They concluded that the merger might be expected to operate against the public interest. Proposing remedies was less easy. National Express could not divest themselves of the coaches as these were owned by other operators; National Express effectively marketed, ticketed, and timetabled the services. In order to prevent adverse effects on the public interest, National Express have had to enter into undertaking with the Director General of Fair Trading:

1. not to increase coach fares above the increased in retail price index (RPI);
2. not to make restrictive changes to terms and conditions for coach tickets, nor to introduced a quote systems for coach tickets, but to maintain the current availability of coach tickets;
3. to provide adequate capacity to meet any current and increased demand for coach services, and to provide not less than the current coach frequencies;
4. to provide a quality of services at least equal to other parts of National Express; and
5. to agree with the DGFT methods of monitoring the above against performance.

National Express were subsequently announced as preferred bidders for North London Railways, Central Trains and ScotRail. All of these acquisitions raise further competition and fair trading issues, although it is unclear whether any further reference to the MMC will be forthcoming.

The London & Continental Connection

After an 18-month competition, the Government announced in February 1996 that the London & Continenal Railways (LCR) consortium had won the right to build the high-speed rail link between London and the Channel Tunnel. As part of this, LCR gained control of European Passenger Services, the UK operator of the Eurostar trains.

The consortium consisted of the following companies (their stakes are shown in brackets):

Bechtel (US) (18%); S G Warburg (UK) (18%); National Express (UK) (17%); Virgin (UK) (17%); Systra (FR) (14%); London Electricity (UK) (12%); Halcrow (UK) (2%); Ove Arup (DK/UK) (2%). This corporate structure is complex, but is supposed to solve some of the problems that occurred during the construction of the Channel Tunnel. The client for the rail line will be the slimmed-down Union Railways, who had designed the line to reference stage.

Staff from Virgin and National Express were quickly installed in order to turn round the loss-making Eurostar business. However, the fire in the Channel Tunnel in November 1996 will not have helped, and whether an improvement in matters can be achieved remains to be seen. Clearly, the successful and profitable operation of the Eurostar trains will be paramount in the successful execution of the high-speed rail link.

In the medium term, however, the operation of services from the British regions will also be important in determining the success of the link. It has always been the intention to operate through services from the Continent to both the East Coast and West Coast Main Lines. The successes of Virgin in winning the West Coast franchise, and of National Express with the Midland Main Line, offer many opportunities to develop feeder services. The joint use of St Pancras station for both domestic and international services would reduce these operators' access charges to Railtrack whilst easing passenger interchange and hence stimulating revenue. These may have been potent considerations in the franchise bids by the two operators.

Sea Containers Ltd

Sea Containers is a transport conglomerate with interests in marine container leasing, ferry, train and port operations, and the leisure industry. It is a company registered and incorporated in Bermuda, and reports quarterly under American reporting conventions. It also had railway experience before franchising. Under the direction of its President, James Sherwood, old Pullman and Wagons Lit carriages had been refurbished to recreate the Venice Simplon Orient Express (VSOE) from London to Venice. Originally hauled by BR locomotives from London to Folkestone, their rolling stock has more recently been used equally for up-market charter and excursion traffic wholly within Britain.

Sea Containers won the East Coast Main Line franchise, with effect from 28th April 1996. They have renamed their franchise Great North Eastern Railway (GNER) and have set about transforming the franchise. The visible appearance of the trains has been considerably altered, with a new livery.

Connex Rail

Connex Rail is the UK rail operating subsidiary of the French CGEA group (Compagnie Generale d'Entreprise Automobiles), which is itself part of the larger Compagnie Generale des Eaux (CGE) group. This is a major diversified conglomeate providing water, service and transport utilities in both the UK and France. In France, they provide infrastructure maintenance services, transport services in 38 urban areas, and operate over SNCF tracks on behalf of both SNCF and local authorities.

Great Western Holdings/ First Bus plc/ 3i Group plc

The management team of BR Great Western Trains, FirstBus plc (see also below) and '3i' Group plc formed a joint venture and won the franchise for the Great Western franchise. FirstBus and 3i each have 24.5% stakes, whilst the management and employeees of Great Western own 51%. The won the franchise to operate from 4th February 1996. The '3i' Group plc – formerly '3i' (Investors In Industry) – is an investment company, and invests in businesses with turnovers between £1 million and £100 million.

Great Western Holdings were subsequently successful in winning the franchise for North West Regional Railways.

FirstBus plc

In December 1996, it was announced that FirstBus plc had won the franchise to operate the Great Eastern franchise from 5th January 1997, on its own (as opposed to being part of a joint venture). FirstBus is a major bus operator with a market capitalisation of £622m in December 1996. It was established in Avon/Somerset, but now has 23 operating subsidiaries throughout Britain.

Company type	Rail operator	Rail operator	Transport operator	Transport operator	Bus operator	Bus operator	Bus operator
Group	Prism Ltd	GB Railways	Sea Containers	National Express	Stagecoach	First Bus	MTL Trust Holdings
Franchises	LTS South West & Wales Cardiff Railway WAGN	Anglia Railways	East Coast Main Line	Midland Mainline Gatwick Express N London Railways Central Trains Scotrail	South West Trains Island Line	Great Eastern	Merseyrail Electrics R R North East
Financial reporting period	1st February 1996 - 12th October 1996		28th April 1996 - 30th September 1996	28th April 1996 - 30th June 1996	4th February 1996 - 12th October 1996		
Turnover	£32.797 million		$179 million	£27.707 million	£191.373 million		
Operating expenses	£32.072 million		$161 million	£27.306 million	£189.273 million		
Exceptional costs	£1.696 million		$11.2 million	£0.401 million	£1.189 million		
Operational profit/loss	£0.971 million		$6.8million		£0.911 million		
% operating profit(+) or loss(-) on turnover	-2.96%		+3.79%	+1.4%	-0.47%		
Notes							

Company type	Bus operator/Utility	Utility conglomerate	Mini - conglomerate	MBO +	MBO +	MBO +	
Group	Go Ahead/Via GTI	CGEA (Connex)	Virgin	MBO = M40 Trains John Laing	MBO=G W Holdings First Bus 3i	MBO=Victory Rlys Go Ahead	
Franchises	Thameslink	Netwk. SouthCentral South Eastern Trains	Cross Country Trains W Coast Main Line	Chiltern Trains	Great Western R R North West	Thames Trains	
Financial reporting period					1st April 1995 - 31st March 1996		
Turnover					£284.5 million		
Operating expenses					£273.4 million		
Exceptional costs							
Operational profit/loss					£11.1 million		
% operating profit(+) or loss(-) on turnover					+3.9%		
Notes					Figures include an apportionment of BR income to 3/2/96		

Table 6.5 Assessment of the Financial Performance of the New Rail Franchisees

GoAhead plc/Thames Trains Ltd

The Go Ahead Group plc is a major bus operator with a market capitalisation of just under £206m in December 1996. It was established in the Newcastle area, but now operates in London, Oxford, High Wycombe and Brighton. They formed a joint venture with the BR management team of Thames Trains. The grouping was given the name Victory Railway Holdings Limited, and were awarded the franchise from 13th October 1996. Go Ahead have a 65% share of Victory, with the remaining 35% owned by the management of Thames Trains.

Go Ahead plc/Via GTI

Go Ahead were also successful in winning the franchise for the Thameslink operation, but this time in consortium with the French company GTI, who have a 35% share. Via GTI are a subsidiary of the group Compagnie de Navigation Mixte (CNM). CNM are a diversified utilities group as well as the largest urban transport operator in France, operating in such cities as Lille. CNM was recently taken over by Banque Paribas.

M40 Trains Ltd/John Laing plc

The award of the franchise for Chiltern Trains was made to the management buy-out team M40 Trains Ltd (74%) supported by John Laing plc (26%). Laings are a major diversified UK construction and engineering group, specialising in house-building. Major projects have included the Second Severn Crossing, and the new Ashford International Railway Station.

MTL Trust Holdings

MTL Trust Holdings has a turnover of £110m p.a. and is one of the major bus operators, based in Merseyside. The group have been successful in securing two franchises: Merseyrail Electrics, and also Regional Railways North East. They intend to go for an AIM listing later in 1997.

Summary

It is now becoming possible to assess the financial position of the new train operating companies; the position as known in December 1996 is set out in Table 6.5. TOCs are unlike many companies. They have few assets, since the trains are leased from the three rolling stock companies. The normal measures for assessing the worth of companies are therefore inappropriate. The simple measure used here is therefore the Operating Profit as measured against the Turnover. Operating Profit has been defined as Turnover – Operating Costs – Exceptional Costs.

From fairly simple calculations based on the available figures, quite some effort will be needed to bring all of the privatised railway franchises into profitability. The table indicates indicative levels of profitability or loss. Studies published by the Financial Times and Sunday Times at the end of October 1996 (Ramesh, 1996; Batchelor, 1996) indicate the significant growth that will be required to achieve this end. The figures take into account Railtrack's track access charges, rolling stock leasing charges and operating costs. Of the 13 franchises analysed, eight would need growth rates significantly higher than 3% p.a. in order to break even. For only some of these do such growth rates look realistic.

Other Companies

Companies supplying *international* rail services (such as EPS) are not subject to regulation; this is different from the situation with Heathrow Express, which is being developed (now wholly by BAA) to operate airport shuttle services to Heathrow, including over Railtrack lines. This is an operation entirely with commercial risk, and was not a service existing before privatisation; other *open-access operators* may appear in due course, but there are complicated rules preventing the introduction of new services until 2002 if these prejudice significant amounts of revenue from an existing TOC. (There are, however, already a number of open-access freight train operators, including National Power, DRS (operating primarily nuclear traffic in the Sellafield area) & Chipman Rail (operating weedkilling trains)).

The three *freight* companies set up as part of the 1993 restructuring were eventually all sold to Wisconsin Central Railroad, and now operate as English, Welsh & Scottish Railways (EWSR); this company also controls the Royal Mail rail operation. Originally named North & South Railways, Wisconsin's subsidiary has continued with the positive developments begun more tentatively with the three previous businesses. The continued development of wagonload freight is certainly one of their avenues for exploration, but so is more traffic all round, with attention being paid to reducing costs in a number of parts of the business. This includes negotiating with Railtrack over possible reductions in track access charges, but also items wholly internal to their business, such as wagon procurement costs and locomotive maintenance. As part of their drive to improve matters, they ordered 250 new locomotives from General Motors within months of their winning the franchise, in order that locomotive reliability could be dragged up to US standards.

Some difficulty was encountered in finding buyers for the Freightliner and Railfreight Distribution companies; the latter, in particular, made significant losses. However, whilst Freightliner was eventually sold to its management, RfD also passed to EW&S. There are clearly economies of scale through incorporating RfD services into EWS.

The three *ROSCOs* own nearly all passenger rolling stock, and also most freight locomotives. The nature of the charging mechanism devised by GATX (the American consultants to the Department of Transport) means that profits here are extremely high, averaging 30% of the £800m turnover across the three companies. Such levels of super-profits inevitably attract the attention of other companies, and direct leasing from rolling stock manufacturers, or ownership by cash-rich operators, seem likely to develop as cheaper alternatives. Indeed, various initiatives are underway to provide competition to the ROSCOs, including the supply of trains to TOCs directly from manufacturers.

In addition, the fleet engineering parts of the business sectors developed into stand-alone organisations known as *TESCOs* (Train Engineering Service Companies). The InterCity business became Interfleet Technology, the NSE business Network Train Engineering Services (NTES) and the Regional/freight business Engineering Link.

Infrastructure Engineering was originally split up into Infrastructure Maintenance Units and Track Renewal Units, each based largely geographically, but with the latter carrying out the larger items of work. Immediate competition became apparent between IMUs and TRUs for intermediate levels of work, whilst their subsequent sale into the private sector led to a number of mergers, some between different functions, and others between the IMU and TRU for the same geographical area. However, genuine competition in this market has emerged, with many of the new companies setting up operating bases outside their core area; for instance, Fastline, with headquarters in York, have a base in London. The market for infrastructure maintenance has progressively been opened up, with an increasing proportion of contracts each year being tendered for competitively.

The Rail Regulators

Three key organisations regulate the industry. *OPRAF* are responsible for administering and supervising the franchising of passenger rail services. Key directions given to the Franchising Director in March 1994 by the Secretary of State were:
- to secure that railway passenger services in Great Britain are provided under franchise agreements as soon as reasonably practicable; and
- to secure an overall improvement in the quality of railway passenger and station services.

In addition, he required OPRAF:
- to encourage efficiency and economy in the provision of railway services;
- to promote the use and cost-effective development of the railway network; and
- to promote the award of franchise agreements to companies in which former British Rail employees have a substantial interest.

The criteria used by OPRAF in drawing up the shortlist of bidders for each TOC were:
- financial position of the tenderer
- managerial competence of the tenderer
- compliance of the bid with the template franchise agreement
- proposed term of franchise
- due diligence requirements

- level of financial support required
- degree of risk transfer proposed
- operational proposals of bidder
- consistency of bids with the Franchising Director's objectives

In practice, OPRAF appeared to favour those with the lowest subsidy, with enhanced, but more expensive bids, not generally being successful. However, the later stages of the franchising process showed some evidence that positive railway development was being looked upon more favourably, in particular that for the West Coast Main Line. OPRAF directly employs around 100 staff, and costs around £15m p.a. to run; this latter figure includes significant payments to various legal and commercial advisors.

The Railway Regulator has a number of key functions, including:
- the issue, modification and enforcement of licences to operate trains, networks, stations and light maintenance depots
- the approval of agreements for access by operators of railway assets to track, stations and light maintenance depots
- the enforcement of domestic competition law; and
- the protection of consumer interests.

Specific (and conflicting) duties noted under section 4 of the Railways Act include:
- the protection of the interests of users of railway services, including the disabled;
- the promotion of the use and development of the national railway network for freight and passengers;
- the promotion of efficiency and economy;
- the promotion of competition;
- through ticketing;
- the minimisation of regulatory burden;
- commercial certainty and security;
- the protection of persons from dangers arising from the operation of the railways, with the advice of the Health and Safety Executive;
- the environmental effect of railway services;

- various statutory guidance from the Secretary of State for Transport;
- the financial position of the Franchising Director and holders of network licences (including Railtrack).

ORR employs around 120 staff, and costs around £10m p.a. to run. A key difference from OPRAF is that (as the joke goes) the Franchising Director does what the Government tells him, whilst the Regulator is independent.

HMRI (the Railway Inspectorate) is an independent safety regulatory body dating from 1840, which was relocated to a position within the Health & Safety Executive as part of the industry restructuring. It has ultimate power in determining the operation of the railway – in extremis, it could close the entire network down on safety grounds. Its inspectors act individually, making formal reports on accidents, and visiting new installations in order to approve them for operation. As a group, they are responsible for validating the overall Railway Safety Case as prepared by Railtrack, whose safety case must ensure that each operator also has a Safety Case. Any of these can be inspected by HMRI, whose role in the operation of the industry is therefore critical.

Local authorities also contribute to the financial costs of running the railways, primarily in terms of revenue support for passenger services, but also for a small number of capital projects. Most important amongst the authorities are the PTEs, operating in the metropolitan areas, and spending £350m p.a. in the new environment. Lack of agreement about the method of this funding led to the temporary withdrawal of Greater Manchester PTE from rail funding, which meant that OPRAF had to step in to maintain service levels, but this issue now appears to have been resolved. However, there remains the anomaly that assets purchased through previous PTE capital expenditure (e.g. in new stations) have now passed to a private-sector company (Railtrack).

Perhaps a hundred other companies also now exist within the railway industry, with the sale of various minor groups previously operating under the 'Central Services' umbrella adding to the fragmentation of the industry. Some of these organisations were described by Madgin (1995). The plethora of organisations has spawned a need for improved industry communication through enhanced advertising, new directories and professional journals and organisations. Consortia of companies are increasingly required to provide all the necessary inputs into large projects, with large engineering-based firms often assisted by smaller specialists.

Impacts on Financial Arrangements

The new organisation described above has two extremely significant impacts on railway financing. First, as more companies become involved in a supplier chain, there is a tendency for prices to rise, as each company takes its slice of profit. These are *interface costs*. For instance, the Franchising Director must pay for the profit 'cut' of a train builder, a ROSCO, a TOC <u>and</u> Railtrack if more trainsets are needed to run an enhanced service. This is only offset by greater efficiency if constituent companies can realise savings through sharing overheads with other contracts (perhaps overseas, or in non-railway sectors) or if the private sector is indeed significantly more efficient than the public sector (which was the underlying, but unproven, philosphy of privatisation in the first place). The long-term solution may be for vertical integration on commercial grounds (a large company might control more profit overall if it took over a chain of supply). This is suggested by the purchase by the Stagecoach group of the Porterbrook ROSCO.

Secondly, there is the potential for *'leakage'* of cash from the new financial regime in a manner not possible in the old system. The old system was described as a 'money-go-round', since various funds (totalling £876m (NAO, 1996)) were effectively recycled – importantly, any profits made by BR or Railtrack went back to the Department of Transport, and could therefore be used (in theory, at least) for further railway expenditure. Once companies are privatised, tax from profits goes to the Treasury, where there is competition for use of the funds from other items of national expenditure (such as the National Health Service) and from macro-economic policy (one might, for instance, use the money to help repay national debt, to reduce the infamous Public Sector Borrowing Requirement). Furthermore, some profit made by private-sector companies is paid as dividends to shareholders, who may have little else to do with the railway industry. Tax may

The Privatisation of British Rail

**The circular cash flow in 1994–95
(at 1994–95 prices)**

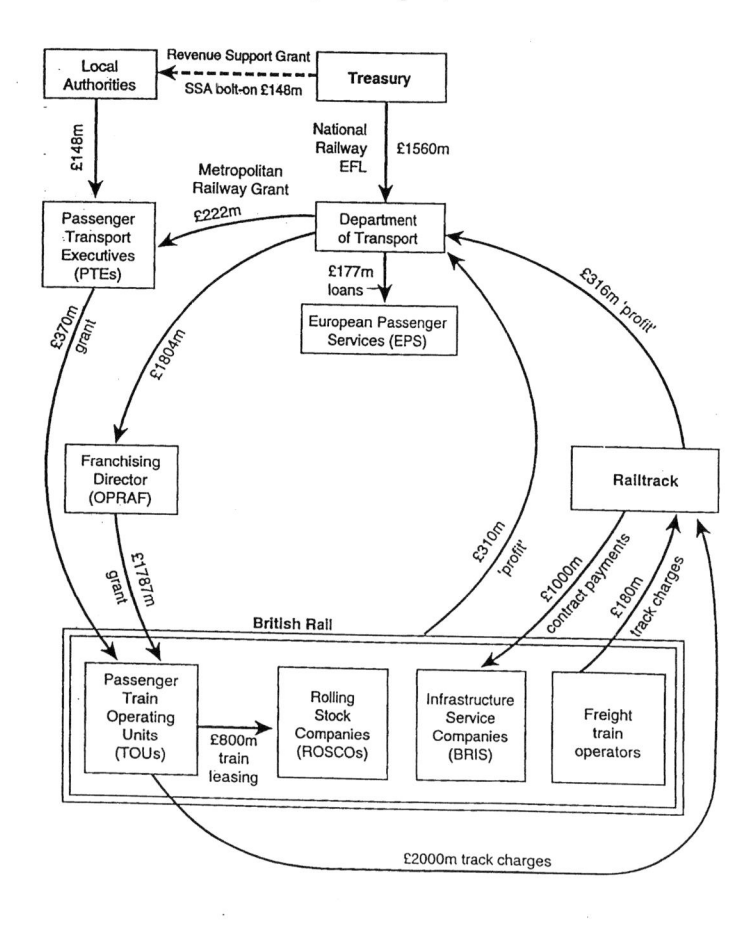

Figure 6.3 Estimated Circular Cash Flow in 1994-5 (at 1994-5 prices)

The New Structure

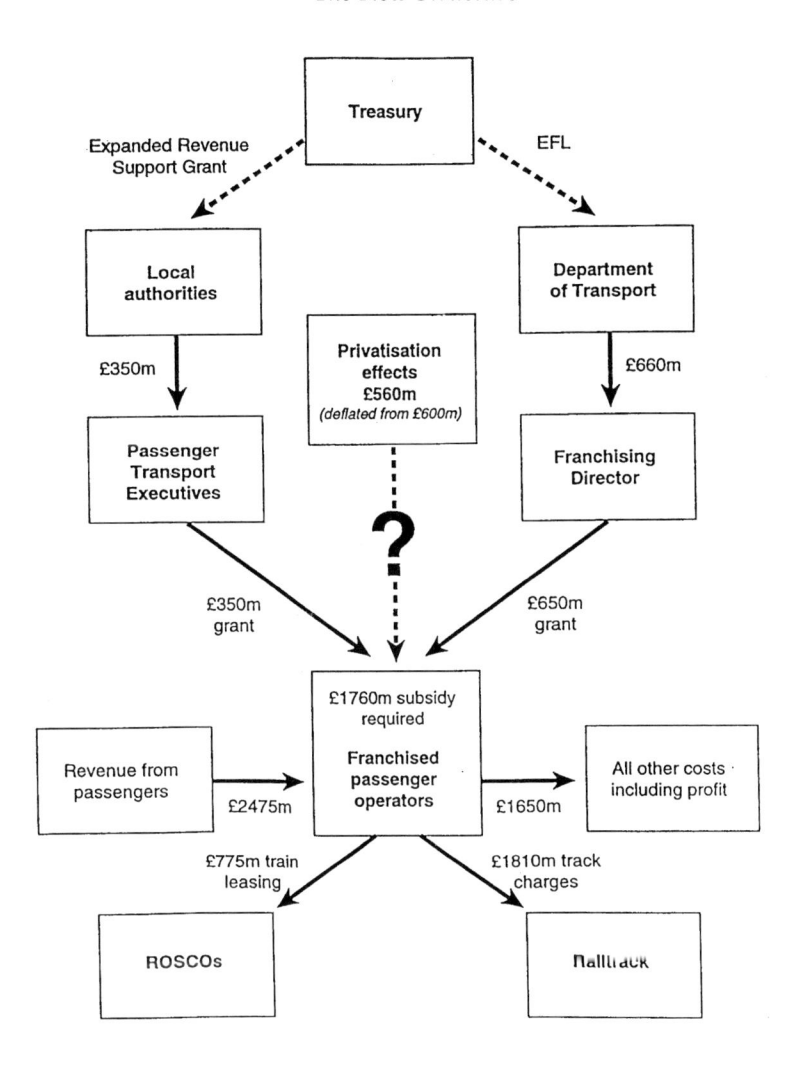

Figure 6.4 Forecast Support for Passenger Services in 1997-8
(at 1994-5 prices)

or may not be paid on these dividends, but is still available to the Treasury for other purposes, as noted above.

These two factors – more profit margins at interfaces, and leakage, were estimated by the Transport Select Committee (HMSO, 1995) to add at least £700m p.a. to railway operating costs in Britain. The financial arrangements for running Britain's railways before and after privatisation are set out in Figures 6.3 and 6.4.

The proportion of a franchise's costs which are controllable is also limited in the current arrangements (typically being around 25% of the total). Franchisees are dependent upon others to provide both infrastructure (Railtrack) and rolling stock (the ROSCOs), a situation which was (unsuccessfully) lobbied against by a number of bidders (including James Sherwood of Sea Containers, and Brian Cox of Stagecoach). The extent of Railtrack's charges can be seen in 'Access Charges' column of Table 6.3, whilst the impact of the ROSCOs can be understood from their annual turnover of around £800m.

Such access charges are levied in three ways. A small charge (around 3% of total) is made for electricity supply, for those services requiring it. Another small element varies with the number of train movements (around 6%), but the vast majority (91%) is fixed across the franchise. The magnitude of this element has been forced downwards through intervention by the Rail Regulator (on an RPI-2% formula, following a one-off 8% reduction in 1995-6) (ORR, 1995), but nevertheless this constitutes a huge fixed cost for franchisees. Conversely, the small marginal element should encourage franchisees to run additional services.

In addition, small variations in performance-related payments may be made under Schedule 8 of the performance agreements between Railtrack and franchisees. If Railtrack fails to deliver the specified train paths, it makes payments to TOCs; if it does better, they pay a premium back. These payments are thought to average £2-3m p.a., falling with time, as Railtrack expects to improve its assets to deliver the paths required. These arrangements took some time to bed down, however, particularly as the monitoring equipment was initially not universally available to support the attribution of delays and hence the payments to be made under Schedule 8.

Impacts on Safety

A number of traffic accidents in 1996 highlighted the importance of the new structure on dealing with operational incidents. A programme of safety initiatives had been instituted by Railtrack since its inception, and these had produced significant safety gains. However, train collisions at Rickerscote (Stafford) and Watford Junction indicated a number of potential problems, as did another incident at Watford when a train overshot the platforms by five miles following a problem with the train brakes. A greater number of managers are now needed to sort out the immediate aftermath of any accident. These interface issues mar what is otherwise impressive progress by Railtrack in increasing railway safety (Railtrack, 1996).

Publicly-available information is certainly less widely-available than previously. No one wishes to admit liability, and these issues are now sorted out (much more slowly!) through lawyers and insurance experts. This can lead to delays at the time, as passengers lose the network benefits of being able to travel by alternative routes, and affected persons may have to wait longer for remedial action (e.g. in the case of the householder in Stafford who landed up with a locomotive resting against his property).

Summary

In summary, the new structure is complicated, and consists of a variety of train operating companies using the facilities of Railtrack as infrastructure provider, under supervision by three regulatory bodies – OPRAF, ORR and HMRI. The operators include a number of bus companies winning passenger franchises, and also some overseas interest. Worries exist about the implications of the number of interfaces between companies, and in subsidy leakage. However, the new system is being made to work.

7 Impacts of the New System – has it Worked?

Introduction

Cynics have alleged that the only beneficiaries of railway privatisation have been paint manufacturers (because of the introduction of new liveries) and insurance salesmen (because of the requirement for the new companies to insure themselves against each other). To the passenger, changes so far have been limited; certainly, few have benefitted as much as commuters on services provided by WAGN from Waltham Cross and Theobald's Grove stations in N E London; these passengers have had their annual Travelcard prices reduced by around £100.

However, it is our intention to provide an objective assessment of privatisation, not the more common anecdotal one. To be objective in judging whether any change has worked, we must identify criteria against which to measure success or failure. Success has certainly been claimed by the Conservative Government, and continues to be claimed – but political success is only one criterion. For railways, other key standards against which to judge the process of fragmentation and privatisation are:

- customer satisfaction
- business efficiency
- wider fiscal efficiency
- general economic efficiency, including
- employment impacts
- environmental impacts
- safety impacts

Each of these are discussed in turn, and the discussion includes consideration of both one-off and continuing changes. We also examine the opportunity costs of privatisation – in other words, what else could have been done with the resources used?

Political Impacts

The political success of railway restructuring and privatisation should be judged by whether those implemented it feel that it has been a net vote-winner or not. Polls conducted during the privatisation process by such groups as Save Our Railways indicated that around 80% of those interviewed were unhappy with either the principle of privatisation, and/or the manner in which it was being carried out. This would tend to indicate that the process was not politically successful. Phrases such as 'poll tax on wheels' also suggest that political commentators felt that rail privatisation was a political liability; whether or not it is a significant factor in the 1997 election remains to be seen. Against a wide range of other economic and political issues, it appears likely that any electoral damage caused by privatising the railways is relatively small, but it cannot have helped the Conservative Government, with its small majority.

On the other hand, privatisation has reduced potential political problems in the future. Future issues in the industry can no longer be seen to be a problem for the Government, since the various industry players can be asked to sort matters out for themselves. Safety can be referred to HMRI, issues of the abuse of monopoly to the Regulator, and financial, subsidy and potential 'fat cat' issues of excessive profit to OPRAF.

Impacts on Customer Satisfaction

British Rail was not renowned for being customer-friendly. Indeed, it was one of those organisations frequently the butt of jokes about being *not* customer-friendly, and this was one of the key reasons prompting privatisation – the private sector was thought to be more customer-orientated. However, the sectorisation of the railways in the late 1980s had already led to a more business-led approach, and service improvements were being made across the sectors. Porters at InterCity stations, more through services, increased staff training, a more pro-active approach to marketing freight by Transrail, and the implementation of charters and standards of punctuality and reliability all helped.

So what happened as a result of privatisation? Freight train operators struggled to provide cost-effective services to potential consignors in the face of enhanced track access charges. New sources of potential complaint for passengers were certainly thrown up with inter-operator problems (such as through and inter-available ticketing) (Wolmar, 1996). Measures of *service performance* also deteriorated throughout the period of change, as demonstrated by statistics provided by the CRUCC (1993-6). It was suggested that performance in the 93-4 year reflected the Organising for Quality initiative, after which the general disruption to the industry, and diversion of management effort towards privatisation issues, led to service deterioration. The figures shown in Table 7.1 may indeed reflect this. However, after new management had settled in, levels of reliability and punctuality often regained their previous levels, and some of the latest figures are promising. Some of the InterCity businesses continued in their quest to improve service quality, with innovations such as 'quiet' coaches on Great Western services, but it would be difficult to argue that these were solely attributable to the private sector's involvement.

	1992-3	1993-4	1994-5	1995-6	1996-7 (6 mths)
Gatwick Express	96.2	90.9	-88.1	89.1	
InterCity East Coast	84.9	89.5	-87.6	86.3	
InterCity CrossCountry	79.4	85.0	-82.6	79.3	
Chiltern	93.7	95.4	-93.6	94.2	94.3
South West outers	88.8	86.5	+87.4	86.0	89.2
SouthCentral outers	85.9	85.9	-84.0	82.4	87.4
South London Lines	88.6	90.3	+90.8	89.6	
ScotRail Central	93.3	92.1	-86.2	90.2	
Northern long-distance	90.7	93.8	+94.9	93.9	
Cardiff Valleys	89.9	93.5	-88.3	90.6	
Lancashire locals	89.6	88.2	-87.4	89.8	
Transpennine	90.7	87.9	+89.7	87.3	

Table 7.1 Train Service Punctuality Levels for a Sample of Key Routes (- indicates a reduction on the previous year, + a gain)

Some of the measures adopted by new companies were largely cosmetic. The repainting of trains, for instance, whilst noticeable to passengers, does not always imply an improved customer service. Evidence from the retail sector shows that improved image not associated with enhanced service can actually 'back-fire', with customer satisfaction levels falling relative to their earlier position. Possible for inclusion in this category were the stations repainted by Connex SouthCentral early in its franchise, some of which became the targets for graffitti vandals.

Impacts of the New System – has it Worked?

Indeed, this highlights the differences that may arise between franchises as variations in unregulated items of service quality are used to reflect cost pressures that TOCs may find themselves under. Particularly strident comparisons regarding the removal of station graffitti soon became noticeable in South London, with some of the stations operated by Thameslink contrasting with neighbouring stations operated by Network SouthCentral. The extent of on-train litter picking was also obviously seen to vary between TOCs, as they took differing views of its cost-effectiveness.

A number of *other products*, which might be regarded by some as marginal, also fell by the wayside. The purchase of all-line 'rover' tickets became more difficult, as no single TOC wished to take responsibility for their administration. Purchase of any tickets at all in Central London became more difficult, as corporate BR offices closed in Victoria and Piccadilly. Policies for offering rebates in cases of late running were sometimes poorer than those offered before privatisation, even if improved punctuality meant that they were needed less often. Some sleeper services did not make it into the PSRs, although that to Fort William survived following considerable public pressure.

The small area of *charter train operation* caused a ripple of excitement at the Office of the Rail Regulator in 1996. For many years, BR had chartered trains, particularly at weekends to enthusiasts and others. The privatisation process started to cause a number of problems, however, due to factors including:

- railway safety case requirements;
- enhanced Railtrack access charges;
- operational problems in working the trains;
- long lead-times to accept charter train bookings;
- last-minute cancellations; and
- invoicing problems.

Parties to the dispute became entrenched in their positions and the Regulator was sought to referee the problem. A reduced number of operators prospered by offering cheaper fares and inducing additional patronage.

A *dearth of investment* in rolling stock during the privatisation process (with 1064 days passing between the orders for Class 365 outer-suburban units for Kent, and Class 166 diesel multiple units for enhanced services out of Marylebone) certainly had an impact in not enhancing passenger in-train environments. However, the increased availability of private sector finance after privatisation did enable considerable investment in some services, with the West Coast Main Line modernisation, and development of freight markets responding to new ownership. In conclusion, customer service undoubtedly suffered during the period 1993-5, but there is considerable hope that future developments will more than counter this. Indeed, if the WCML programme actually delivers what it is capable of, with 25% journey time savings to Manchester, and frequencies doubled, this will probably outweigh any temporary failings in service. However, where new owners have concentrated on cost-saving, rather than growing the market, customer benefits are not apparent. A geographical variation in customer satisfaction is therefore inevitable, even if the overall picture is positive in the longer-term.

Franchise Efficiency

Any assessment of franchise efficiency involves determining whether or not the output of the railways has been achieved more or less cheaply in the new structure than under the old. In a steady-state situation in the private sector, earning per share can provide a useful guide to performance, but the expansion of companies into rail franchising makes this comparison impossible.

Improvements in railway efficiency can, of course, accrue from three sources. There may be *operational improvements* – can the assets be made to work harder? Can enhanced service quality attract and retain additional (especially offpeak) patronage? Such improved quality can also accrue from *enhanced investment* levels. However, there are also wider issues of *economic efficiency*, and these are the contentious ones. Will assets be stripped? Will network developments or entirely new products extend the market? A simple analysis of franchise payments can only examine these three types of efficiency together, but we can make an indicative appraisal of the relative importance of all three types within the different businesses.

Moreover, there may be trade-offs in efficiency; for instance, a new system might provide slightly more railway but at a slightly higher price. This can, however, be evaluated through a measure such as output per input.

Impacts of the New System – has it Worked?

But what are the outputs of a railway? The correct measure of railway supply is train miles (or, better, vehicle miles), but this takes no account of whether the supply is useful (remember that transport demand is time-dependent), or of what quality (late trains are worth less than punctual ones). For the freight sector, without public subsidy, costs per tonne-km are critical. BR's performance was reasonably poor over the period 1990-5, with costs per train-mile remaining broadly constant (BRB, 1995; information on train length not available). However, new owners EW&S Railways undertook to increase freight traffic volumes, partly through efficiency gains in areas such as administration, locomotive maintenance and materials (Burkhardt, 1997).

For a passenger railway, we are probably interested in delivering passenger miles, although this varies with other factors such as network extent and (more critically) the overall state of the economy. Fortunately for this analysis, changes in network extent and economic activity were pretty limited in the period of interest; slight economic growth was offset by strikes in the Summer of 1994. As a first cut, we therefore need to examine the following ratio:

Passenger miles
Total input payments

However, the definition of total input payments is also not entirely straightforward. Subsidies from both local and central Government clearly need to be included, but so does passenger revenue. This might change as a result of fares increases, in addition to changes due to inflation, which we can correct for.

Year	Pass. Jnys (m)	Revenue Grant (£m)	Total Grant (£m)	Rev. Grant/jny (£)
1991-2	741	524	1104	0.71
1992-3	745	704	1354	0.94
1993-4	713	545	2173	0.76
1994-5	702	2060	2169	2.93
1995-6	719	1983	2059	2.76

Table 7.2 Impact of the New Railway Structure on Industry Finances

Notes: Total grant includes capital grants, and contributions from PTEs. Freight operations have been excluded, as they are subject to minimal grant.

Sources: BRB Annual Reports and Accounts.

In fact, table 7.2 suggests that fares increases and inflation are of negligible importance when compared to the changes in railway finances necessitated by the introduction of the new industry structure. Total grant broadly doubled over the period, whilst revenue grant increased even more steeply. (Figures for immediately-preceding years, whilst not entirely comparable, demonstrate even lower grant requirements). Several billion pounds have therefore been spent on the transition to the new system. Forecasts for future grant requirements for franchises suggest a reduction to £500m is only reached in 2011-12. The full details of these changes are calculated later in this chapter, but the immediate conclusion is that the business efficiency of the railway certainly suffered during the change-over period from the public to the private sector.

Analysis of Franchise Bids

As we have seen, improvements in "efficiency" can be at one of two levels – a narrow operational level, or a wider economic level, either of which may be underpinned by investment. Operational improvements are exemplified by the more effective use of rolling stock, as with GNER's use of the 28th East Coast trainset on Fridays, by adjusting maintenance schedules. Economic efficiency may occur either in a negative sense (e.g. through asset stripping) or market growth. Fortunately, the political debate in passing the Act foresaw the potential for asset stripping, probably because the sale of bus stations had been a marked example of it in the bus privatisation programme of recent years. If there are no economic factors at work, then any improvement in business performance reflected by bids for less subsidy must come from operational issues.

In the 1980s, BR concentrated on cutting costs. At the time, costs on the railways were often around three times revenues, and a 10% reduction in costs was therefore more significant than a 10% increase in revenue. In the conditions of the 'new' railway, however, costs have been reduced, whilst around two-thirds of them are outside the control of the TOCs anyway. With 40% of a franchise's costs typically going in access payments to Railtrack, and another 25% to ROSCOs, there is relatively little room for cost-cutting within a franchise (on top of the reductions in

Railtrack access charges imposed by the Regulator). Greater potential within franchises is generally through revenue growth.

Some of the franchises clearly have more potential for market expansion than others. For instance, Chiltern Railways' plans to compete with others in the London-Birmingham market make a considerable impact on their finances, but probably only a small impact on that of the bigger InterCity West Coast business. On the other hand, Island Line probably has limited room for manouevre. This means that any forecast improvements as demonstrated by the bids set out in Table 7.3 and Figure 7.1 must come primarily from operational improvements – taking on board reductions in Railtrack track access charges, increased competition between IMUs for minor maintenance, and so on. Note that it is not possible to attempt an analysis of the change in revenue alone, since requirement for subsidy depends upon both costs and revenues, and cost reductions of varying levels are also to be expected.

Franchise Turnround

We have examined the improvement in business performance across all the TOCs, in terms of the turnround they have subscribed to during their franchise. We have calculated the change in the ratio of costs to passenger revenue at the beginning and end of the franchise period, assuming that revenues stay the same in real terms (see Table 7.4). Great West Trains shows an improvement in performance of around 11%, but this is actually less than the reduction in Railtrack's track access charges imposed by the Regulator, which come to round 20%. Let us suppose that this is indeed what the private sector can deliver in terms of increased operational efficiency (and perhaps what ex-BR managers could have done, within their restricted ambit).

A number of the other TOCs are committed to the introduction of new trains or (as in the case of Thames and Chiltern) have recently received them. Past research shows that new trains can generate up to 10% additional revenue and, if more efficient, can lead to savings in leasing costs. This could lead to a reduction in subsidy of 15%, even without important secondary impacts such

£M	1996-7	1997-8	1998-9	1999-00	2000-1	2001-2	2002-3	2003-4	2004-5	2005-6	2006-7	2007-8	2008-9	2009-10	2010-11	2011-2
SWT	-54.7	-54.7	-53.6	-49.9	-46.5	-43.3	-40.3	0.0	0.0	0.0	0.0	0.0	0.0	0.0	0.0	0.0
GWT	-53.2	-49.9	-46.8	-42.5	-38.6	-36.9	-35.2	-33.6	-32.6	-31.6	-31.6	-31.6	-31.6	-31.6	-31.6	-31.6
LT&S	-29.5	-26.6	-24.0	-22.5	-21.1	-19.9	-18.6	-17.5	-16.4	-15.4	-14.5	-13.6	-12.8	-12.0	-11.2	-11.2
ICEC	-56.9	-64.6	-51.0	-32.0	-12.7	-3.7	-1.8	0.0	0.0	0.0	0.0	0.0	0.0	0.0	0.0	0.0
GatEx	3.9	4.6	6.2	7.9	9.7	10.5	11.2	11.7	13.0	14.4	15.9	16.4	17.9	19.4	21.0	22.6
NSC	-93.0	-85.3	-69.6	-48.9	-43.9	-40.8	-36.7	-34.6	-34.6	-34.6	-34.6	-34.6	-34.6	-34.6	-34.6	-34.6
MML	-16.5	-6.3	-1.0	-0.2	1.6	2.6	4.4	6.2	8.1	10.1	10.0	10.0	10.0	10.0	10.0	10.0
Chiltern	-16.5	-13.0	-11.9	-8.6	-5.6	-4.1	-2.9	-2.9	-2.9	-2.9	-2.9	-2.9	-2.9	-2.9	-2.9	-2.9
SE	-120.8	-125.4	-97.7	-65.0	-52.8	-42.1	-36.0	-26.8	-26.8	-18.7	-18.7	-12.5	-9.5	-5.7	0.0	2.8
SW&W	-80.0	-70.9	-60.5	-55.9	-50.0	-46.3	-42.9	-38.1	-38.1	-38.1	-38.1	-38.1	-38.1	-38.1	-38.1	-38.1
CV	-21.5	-19.9	-17.6	-16.6	-15.4	-14.6	-13.9	-13.3	-13.3	-13.3	-13.3	-13.3	-13.3	-13.3	-13.3	-13.3
Island	-2.0	-1.9	-1.8	-1.8	-1.8	-1.8	-1.8	-1.8	-1.8	-1.8	-1.8	-1.8	-1.8	-1.8	-1.8	-1.8
Thames	-38.7	-33.2	-24.0	-16.5	-13.1	-7.4	-3.7	0.0	0.0	0.0	0.0	0.0	0.0	0.0	0.0	0.0
Xcountry	-126.7	-112.9	-95.5	-80.0	-72.0	-66.0	-49.2	-38.4	-21.5	-13.4	-6.9	-3.0	-0.8	0.0	5.0	10.0
GE	-40.6	-29.0	-14.0	-8.1	-2.8	0.3	5.1	9.5	9.5	9.5	9.5	9.5	9.5	9.5	9.5	9.5
WAGN	-71.1	-52.9	-33.8	-24.7	-12.7	-4.2	14.2	24.8	24.8	24.8	24.8	24.8	24.8	24.8	24.8	24.8
Anglia	-40.9	-35.9	-26.0	-22.1	-16.0	-13.0	-8.6	-6.3	-6.3	-6.3	-6.3	-6.3	-6.3	-6.3	-6.3	-6.3
Merseyrail*	-81.5	-80.7	-72.8	-67.2	-64.9	-62.0	-61.6	-60.8	-60.8	-60.8	-60.8	-60.8	-60.8	-60.8	-60.8	-60.8
NWRR*	-185.1	-184.9	-168.9	-153.4	-140.8	-134.8	-129.7	-125.5	-125.5	-125.5	-125.5	-125.5	-125.5	-125.5	-125.5	-125.5
N London	-50.0	-48.6	-35.5	-29.6	-26.4	-23.0	-20.0	-16.9	-16.9	-16.9	-16.9	-16.9	-16.9	-16.9	-16.9	-16.9
RRNE*	-215.4	-224.5	-197.1	-175.8	-164.3	-156.3	-150.5	-145.6	-145.6	-145.6	-145.6	-145.6	-145.6	-145.6	-145.6	-145.6
Thlink	-11.1	-2.5	6.7	16.2	22.5	23.2	27.0	28.4	28.4	28.4	28.4	28.4	28.4	28.4	28.4	28.4
Central*	190.5	-187.5	-173.4	-153.7	-145.8	-140.9	-136.6	-132.6	-132.6	-132.6	-132.6	-132.6	-132.6	-132.6	-132.6	-132.6
WCML	-73.47	-76.8	-68.4	-56.1	-53.7	-52.3	3.9	52.7	55.8	72.0	126.6	151.6	167.6	184.5	202.2	220.3
ScotRail*	-281.1	-280.1	-264.8	-250.5	-234.9	-220.4	-209.3	-202.5	-202.5	-202.5	-202.5	-202.5	-202.5	-202.5	-202.5	-202.5
TOTAL	-1946.8	-1863.5	-1596.6	-1341.3	-1202.0	-1097.1	-933.4	-763.8	-738.5	-700.8	-637.4	-600.9	-577.4	-553.5	-522.7	-495.2

*: inc PTE

Underlined figures are as paid to BR; note that 1995-6 equivalent payments for the six franchises back to OPRAF
+ve values are payments from franchisees back to OPRAF   Italicised figures are projections
Underlined figures are as paid to BR; note that 1995-6 equivalent payments for the six franchises without BR figures were £100,000 less than the 1996-7 figures. Payments for years beyond the franchise have been maintained at the level of that in the last year, except for SWT where a zero net payment has been assumed

Table 7.3 *Passenger Franchise Payments (source: OPRAF press releases)*

Impacts of the New System – has it Worked?

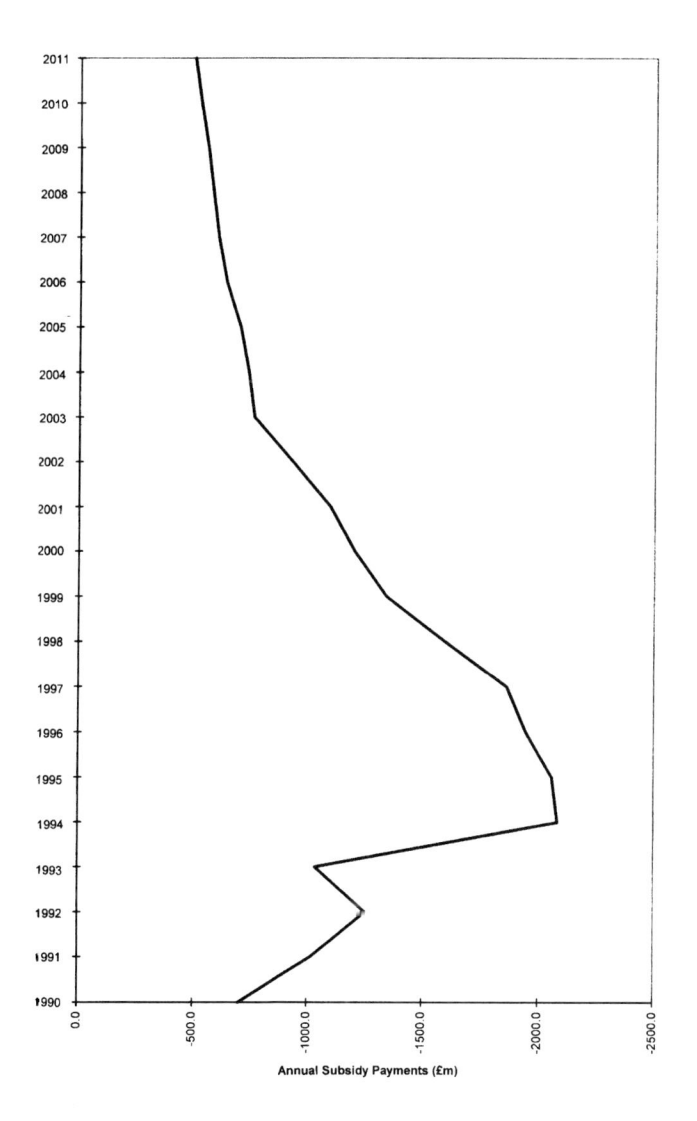

Figure 7.1 Government Expenditure on Rail Passenger Services 1990-2012

as increases in service frequency which the new rolling stock might enable. If this is the case, any further improvements in financial performance (as demonstrated by reductions in subsidy) are due to wider economic effects, such as "growing the market".

The Privatisation of British Rail

Franchise	Business Turnround % change over franchise	
SouthWest Trains	19	
Great West Trains	11	
LT&S	23	P1
InterCity East Coast	22	
Gatwick Express	80	
Network SouthCentral	23	
Midland Main Line	35	
Chiltern	35	
South East Trains	37	
South Wales & West	35	P2
Cardiff Valleys	30	P3
Island Line	10	
Thames Trains	45	
CrossCountry	60	
Great Eastern	33	
WAGN	54	P4
Anglia	46	
Merseyrail	21	
NWRR	26	
N London Railways	32	
RRNE	25	
Thameslink	52	
Central	23	
WCML	101	
ScotRail	21	

Table 7.4 Improvements in Business Efficiency Offered by Winning Franchises
P = won by Prism (for explanation see text)

The fact that a number of the TOCs seem to have signed up for turnrounds of around 35% is interesting. We can infer from this that market expansion is worth up to 20% extra, on top of the forecast improvements in operational efficiency, and in addition to the impact of new trains. This is borne out by examining those franchises with the highest proportionate improvements (Gatwick Express, Cross Country and WCML). These perhaps have the most potential for aggressive marketing to increase their market share.

However, a franchise with a low proportionate improvement is South West Trains, with only a 19% turnround assumed. Of this, a significant proportion (perhaps half) is solely due to the imposed reductions in Railtrack access charges. The low overall turnround is despite apparent room for growth in some of the leisure and business markets offered between London and Southampton, Bournemouth and Dorset. A number of commentators have suggested that Stagecoach were not committed to market expansion, but as a company had a reputation for cost cutting (i.e. the operational efficiency element). A lack of market expansion might reflect recent trends in the bus industry; market share there has also been falling. The evidence, though, shows that Stagecoach is not alone in having limited targets for improvement. In fact, the earlier franchises generally show less business improvement than the latter. Put another way, to win one of the later franchises, one had to promise greater improvements in business performance. Chiltern's business case, for instance, required a 60% increase in revenue; Stagecoach's for SWT clearly did not. We have graphed improvement in business performance against the date of franchise letting, which does tend to support this theory.

Other evidence supports this suggestion. Table 7.4 shows how Prism's four winning bids (marked P1–P4) have required increasing turnrounds; 23% was enough to win LT&S, but 54% was needed at WAGN. A number of commentators have also suggested that, had the SWT franchise been let nearer the end of the franchise programme (rather than being the first one), the winning bid would have needed to have demonstrated payments back to the Franchising Director. However, as OPRAF's main objective was to get the franchising programme off to a successful start, they were probably not unduly worried, whilst the National Audit Office carried out an investigation of OPRAF's initial performance (NAO, 1996) and were generally satisfied. We can therefore be sure that increased optimism has been required to win subsequent bids.

Some of the PTE bids, however, are effectively different from the main batch because revenue risk is retained by the PTE. That element of business turnround accounted for by market growth is therefore missing. The fact that the overall business turnround is

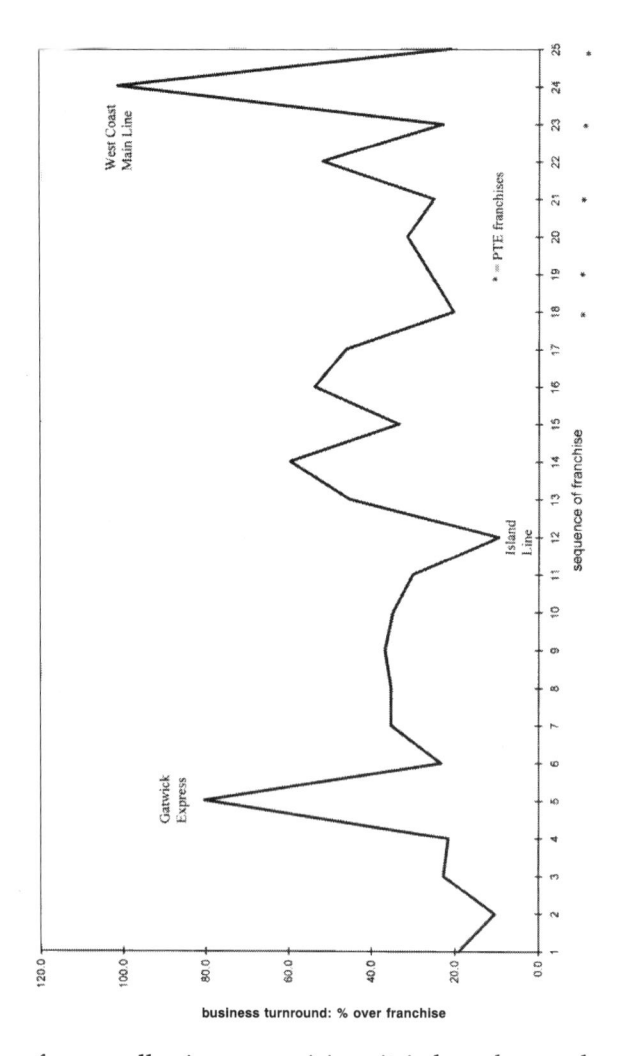

Figure 7.2 Franchise Business Turnround and Date of Franchise Letting

therefore smaller is unsurprising; it is based on only part of the business (the cost side).

It is also interesting to find out how bids compared with each other. If the winning bid was significantly better than the others, this might demonstrate a genuinely novel approach – or an error in the bidder's calculations. The NAO showed that indicative bids for LTS, Great Western and South West Trains ranged between

Impacts of the New System – has it Worked?

New livery: Detail of Connex branding
on Class 455 no. 5804 at London Victoria [N.G. Harris]

New livery: GWT-reliveried HST set at Paddington
[N.G. Harris]

*Station refurbishment at Gipsy Hill,
on the Connex SouthCentral network [N.G. Harris]*

*New livery: 56058 in EW&S livery at Peterborough
[E.W. Godward]*

£155-£188m, £252-417m and £298-639m respectively (all figures being the total subsidy payable over the term of the franchise). The variation in the bids for South West Trains is particularly noteworthy, since the business turnround offered by the winner has proved to be relatively low – were there really few opportunities for cost reduction or revenue growth? Clearly, the independent consultant advising OPRAF thought so – but he did not have the advantage of the experience which is now available.

In the end, OPRAF did not take forward some earlier suggestions about sharing revenue risk with franchise bidders. Risk has remained solely with the private sector, and is presumably higher with the later and more ambitious bids. OPRAF's main risk is in respect of the corporate failure of one of the bidders.

So, in summary, how is business efficiency to improve? Clearly, Railtrack's access charges are to fall. New trains will increase revenue and reduce costs, especially as some of these proposals involve the replacement of locomotive-hauled carriages with multiple-unit stock. Increases in train service frequency are also likely to generate demand; Virgin's prospects for CrossCountry seem likely to produce the same sort of impacts that 'Sprinterisation' of many Regional inter-urban services did in the period 1988-93. Patronage on the North Transpennine between Leeds and Manchester is thought to have risen by 70% in this period, so perhaps Virgin's projections of a doubling in demand on Cross Country services are not unduly optimistic. It may be that revenue growth will be limited in those franchises won by bus operators, in contrast to the proposals by Virgin, who are a more marketing-led organisation.

Some franchises are promising increases in journey speed – e.g. on the West Coast Main Line, and Midland Main Line. In the case of the latter, however, this will partly be achieved by the separation of fast and slow services to provide a two-tier service (with frequency increased in total). Sheffield will benefit from faster services to London; intermediate stations will benefit from more frequent (if slower) services.

Reductions in administration and other overheads were shown very early on to be targets for those winning franchises, as Stagecoach made 750 redundancies within weeks of taking over at

The Privatisation of British Rail

SWT. This included 125 head office and administrative staff. Whether these posts were genuinely spare, or whether they can only be dispensed with in the short term, remains to be seen.

The cost-cutting approach was soon shown to have disadvantages, however. Stagecoach were fined by OPRAF in February 1997 for an undue number of train cancellations on SWT, because too many drivers had been released for voluntary severance.

Marketing initiatives have not only focussed on price, but also on wider aspects of the service, including integration with other modes. A number of operators have introduced bus or coach links to their services, in order to widen their catchment areas. This was perhaps less surprising with Stagecoach (with buses connecting Romsey to Winchester), but perhaps more so for Great North East Railways (with a coach service linking Lincoln with Newark, and thereby competing with the Regional Railways service). Data for their forecast business turnround is graphed as Figure 7.3.

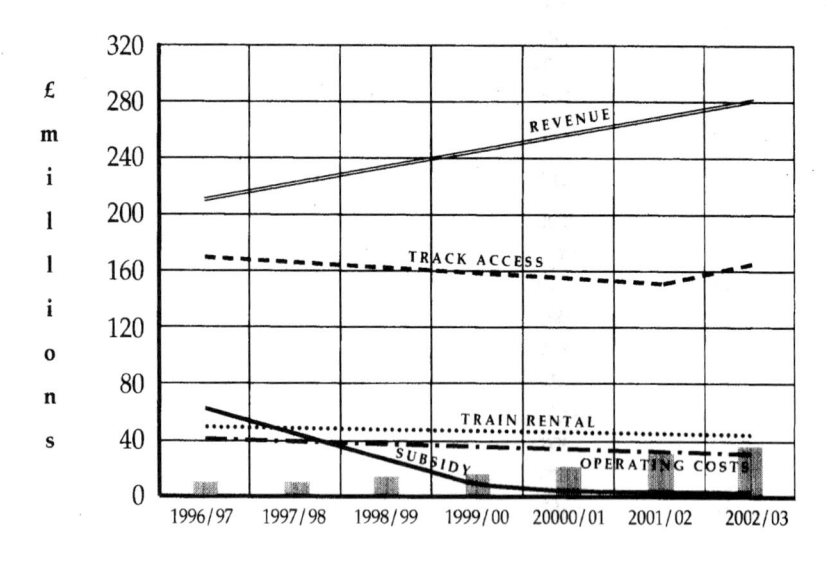

Figure 7.3 Franchise Turnround for Great North East Railways

Columns show the budgetted increase in profit.
Profit is revenue + subsidy − track access, train rental and operating costs.

Impacts of the New System – has it Worked?

In summary, operational efficiency improvements, new trains and market growth are the three main factors driving the forecast improvement in business performance of the TOCs. In addition, later franchises were more competitive, and better bids were needed to secure them.

Overall Fiscal Efficiency – Initial Impacts

There is little point at rejoicing in the improved business efficiency of individual TOCs if the overall fiscal cost to the country has risen. We have therefore carried out an analysis to examine this issue. Two perspectives need to be taken on the assessment. In particular, the wider costs to Great Britain plc need to be distinguished from the narrower financial impacts on the Government. This distinction is most marked when considering tax implications which, in the wider view of matters, are merely transfer payments, and do not represent any benefit or disbenefit to society as a whole.

Any analysis of the benefits of privatisation also needs to examine the costs of the change itself. There would be no financial point in privatising an industry if the costs of doing so outweighed the cost savings afterwards.

Intrinsically, the net impact of the privatisation of any industry needing continuing support can be estimated by considering the one-off costs and benefits of the privatisation process itself with the ongoing costs and benefits. Government would hope that the ongoing benefits would provide the rationale for the process, by exceeding in magnitude the costs typically associated with the process itself. True comparisons have been made in this case by bringing all costs and benefits to the current year, and making a comparison on an NPV basis. A discount rate of 8% has been assumed in calculations; this may, however, be high at present, given current interest rates. A lower discount rate might reduce the benefits of a privatisation, because the anticipated savings accrue after the costs of the privatisation process itself. Work by White (1996a) indicates that a drop in the discount rate to 6% could reduce the financial benefits of privatisation by around £1bn.

Initial Costs

The set-up costs associated with a programme of privatisation should not be under-estimated, particularly as the individuals involved in the process are usually expensive professionals in the legal, accountancy and management consultancy disciplines. A Parliamentary reply quoted in Hansard of 15/11/96 indicated that £450m had already been spent on management, legal and accountancy consultancy advice during the privatisation of the mainline rail businesses. Table 7.5 sets out the *known* costs by company and year, in £m p.a..

Organisation	1992-3	1993-4	1994-5	1995-6
DoT/ORR/OPRAF	5.5	12.4	27.3	51.7
British Rail	0	92	85	101
Railtrack	0	0	46	32
Total	5.5	104.4	158.3	184.7

Table 7.5 Known Expenditure on Consultancy during the Rail Privatisation Process
Source: Modern Railways, Jan 1997 p. 12.

Other costs (including redundancy costs, remaining costs, and the bidding costs incurred by potential purchasers and franchisees) bring this to an estimated £1.2bn. These costs were the subject of a report by the National Audit Office (1996), which also indicated a figure of over £1bn. The reason for such a high figure is that the method selected for privatising BR was particularly complicated, with an estimated 96 separate companies being created. Staff within the industry were paid to relocate – or accept redundancy. Offices were moved, new computer systems set up, and old organisations split up and transferred.

Some set-up costs are independent of the number of companies created; a notional figure for such costs has been estimated at £50m. Other costs, however, *are* dependent on the number of companies created; on the basis of the evidence available, these appear to be around £12m per company created. However, that does not replicate the number of inter-company transactions, which are the real cause of costs (as legal agreements need to be set up to replace the "Gentleman's Agreements" which previously existed). The £450m figure noted above should therefore be considered against the number of inter-company contracts (perhaps 30,000 in the BR case).

As we have already seen, service performance fell during the period of change. This can be attributed to management attention being diverted away from the key objective of running trains to other issues – perhaps including mounting management buy-outs (MBOs). Broadly, 2% of trains failed to arrive within their five-minute targets, over and above the ongoing norm for punctuality as seen both before and after privatisation. Even if this only involved 2% of trains being 5.5 minutes late, rather than 4.5 minutes late, this constitutes a significant disbenefit. There are around 1bn passenger boardings on BR services p.a. (as some journeys involve boarding more than one train). We estimate this as being worth one minute for 2% of the 1bn boardings p.a. which, with a Value Of Time of £5/hour, suggests a disbenefit to society of around £2m during the transition process. Similar calculations show the disbenefit from the increased number of cancellations to exceed £1m. Note that these disbenefits are actually quite small.

Sale Proceeds

A politically-important category of benefits are the proceeds of sales of the businesses in the industry being privatised. The values of the sales of Railtrack, ROSCOs, EWS (freight) and other, miscellaneous, businesses have been taken from various published sources. Railtrack is known to have fetched around £1.9bn, the ROSCOs £1.8bn, and the freight and parcels businesses perhaps £325m. Over £150m was raised from sales of the IMCs and TRCs, even if this appeared to be very cheap compared to their turnovers. A further £132m was raised from the sale of BR Telecoms to Racal, but the large number of remaining businesses only fetched about £140m (see Appendix A).

Adjustments to Initial Costs and Benefits

The above summary of costs and benefits does not, however, provide a complete picture of the impact on the Government of a privatisation programme. A number of figures are required to give an indication of the types of adjustment which should properly be included. First, a value should be placed on the losses incurred on the sale, since this should be charged to a (nominal UK plc) balance sheet. The book value of Railtrack was quoted as £4.3bn but the sale price achieved was £1.9bn. £2.4bn was therefore 'lost' to the economy. In fact, this is a minimum estimate, since Railtrack's asset book value of £4.3bn is undoubtedly less than the replacement cost – a figure of £10bn might be more appropriate. Depending upon the accounting conventions used, zero book values are sometimes used for 'sunk' costs such as tunnels, although these clearly have potential for wider (or, indeed, alternative) uses, and do indeed have an intrinsic value.

It is also reasonable to assume that the sale prices of the IMCs and TRCs were also too low. When their sale prices are examined against their annual turnover, it is clear that some of them were sold for only 10% of their annual turnover. For a normal company making a 10% profit margin, this implies that purchasers were only paying for one year's profits, thereby discounting completely any future for the companies. Higher sale prices should undoubtedly have been reached here; we have made an estimate of a notional £50m. (Indeed, this reflects a more general trend that the BR Privatisation Unit was markedly less successful in selling businesses off as a whole than was OPRAF in franchising the passenger business).

Four smaller adjustments are also required when estimating the net effect of privatising the pieces of BR. Railtrack's profits of £69m made during its public ownership were actually transferred to the private sector, whilst £1229m of debts were written off. The loss-making Freightliner and Railfreight Distribution businesses were sold with 'sweeteners' (e.g. in track access grants paid by Government) thought to be around £75m and £500m respectively. Lastly, the liabilities associated with the upkeep of 1000 bridges were transferred to local authorities; a nominal estimate of £1bn should be allocated for these, at a per-bridge value of £1m.

In order to complete an objective assessment, we must also consider what are termed *opportunity costs*. In other words, what else could have been done with the resources used in privatisation? Limiting ourselves to the railway industry (since comparisons across industries would make matters horrendously complicated), on what else could a Government have spent the transition costs of £1.2bn?

A number of suggestions for alternative expenditure were made during the process itself. Foremost amongst these was the cost of upgrading the West Coast Main Line, linking London with Birmingham, Manchester, Liverpool and Glasgow at a cost of

Impacts of the New System – has it Worked?

around £700m (at the time). This would not only have provided significant financial benefits to the railway industry per se, but has a large impact on mode choice across much of Britain; large-scale transfers of traffic to rail might be expected from such a scheme, with attendant environmental benefits. We have not seen the detailed financial analysis for this scheme but, on the basis that it is financially viable, its net financial impact must be around £70m p.a. Assuming that the scheme enables a number of operating cost savings to offset the additional train miles envisaged, it may generate £70m p.a. of revenue, and passenger benefits of perhaps £150m.

In a similar vein, the Thameslink project for linking services North and South of the Thames was also delayed as a result of privatisation, and could have been funded earlier (at an approximate cost of £300m in 1993). This too would have had significant financial and social benefits – even if regional in nature.

Progress in developing light rail systems was also delayed for a lack of finance, although the benefits of schemes such as those in Manchester and Sheffield were not seriously questioned. Meanwhile, schemes in Croydon, Nottingham and elsewhere (costing the Government around £100m each) proceeded more slowly – or not at all. Many potential minor railway improvements could also have been brought forward by a Government with a more pro-active approach to developing the railway network. In conclusion, then, there were indeed other schemes with benefits delayed because of privatisation. As an order of magnitude, since transport expenditure is not authorised unless benefits exceed 1.3 times costs, the benefits of £1.2bn spent within the industry would have been expected to reach £2bn across the life of the projects. Financial analysis therefore shows that a delay of three years to these benefits is worth broadly £425m, which may be seen to be the opportunity costs of privatisation. Clearly, if any projects were deferred indefinitely as a result of privatisation (rather than just for three years), this figure could be even higher.

Unfortunately, other demands for funds have gone unheeded as a result of the money spent on privatisation. Within the railway, the £850m p.a. extra annual cost of operating the system can be compared to such schemes as the cancelled system-wide introduction of ATP signalling equipment (£600m) or the Channel Tunnel Rail Link (at £3bn).

Overall Fiscal Efficiency – Ongoing Impacts

Ongoing Costs

Although a prime objective of privatisations is to yield ongoing benefits, the process also adds costs to the Exchequer if industries need ongoing financial support. Irrespective of the manner of privatisation, a profit margin needs to be added in, one the basis that such a margin is the business objective of any purchaser or lessee. 10% of turnover might be typical. However, if the industry is split into more elements, more than one profit margin may be added to the final bill. For instance, a track maintenance company may add its profit margin to its supplies to the infrastructure authority, who add their profit margin to their charge to the Train Operating Company, who in turn add their mark-up to the subsidy requested from Central Government. Further administrative costs also arise at the margin, with legal and compliance monitoring costs to be added to the profit margins at these inter-company interfaces. Yet more Government subsidy is needed to cover for these *interface* costs. Hansard of 17/4/96 indicates that subsidies of £930m from Central Government plus £105m from PTEs in financial year 1993/4 necessarily rose to £1740m and £340m respectively in year 1994/5. However, our analysis has used another published estimate, of £850m p.a.

Regulatory and service specification costs for the mainline railway network (incurred by ORR and OPRAF respectively) amounted to £26m p.a. in 1994-5, which appears to be a typical year, given forecasts of expenditure of these bodies as presented in the 'Red Book' which accompanied the 1996 Budget.

The introduction of company interfaces also has impacts on passengers. Negative consequences can occur both with both investment issues (Harris, 1994) and operating issues. Problems can arise with joint investment in projects, since all parties need a return; the project is driven by that participant with the lowest return. On the operating side, it would appear that, even with the intervention of the Regulator, it is impossible to prevent some inter-company issues (e.g. through-ticketing, information) developing into problems for the passenger.

To an order of magnitude, we can estimate the social disbenefits of such problems. For instance, around 200 million passengers make journeys involving an interchange each year. Supposing that, on average, each of those changes became more onerous by one minute (e.g. because of additional requirements in finding out information, or having their tickets checked twice, or having to rebook, in order to take advantage of particularly-favourable ticket offers). Since we have some idea of the value which passengers place on their time (around £5/hour, on average), we can value this time – on these assumptions, it would be approximately £17m p.a. Any such figure for benefit loss must logically exceed any revenue actually lost from such annoyances, because some passengers, whilst inconvenienced, still travel and pay the fare. Such a revenue loss is included within the net change in subsidy required by the franchisee, and is therefore not estimated separately here, in order to avoid double-counting.

In fact, the potential for revenue loss at the interfaces between operators was identified at an early stage as a matter of concern, and a preliminary estimate of its magnitude was made by SDG (1993). They forecast that perhaps £45m p.a. could be lost; on the basis that benefit losses are typically three times greater than revenue losses, we have therefore taken a benefit loss of £135m p.a.

Ongoing Benefits

A key underlying idea of privatisation is that private-sector companies can deliver goods and services more cheaply than the public sector, for a variety of reasons. Cheaper and easier access to capital for investment may be a particularly important reason for a railway, which requires a substantial and sustained investment programme. Franchisees would be expected to deliver services for less subsidy than the public-sector equivalent; we have already seen that the average reduction in subsidy is around 30% of turnover, with greater improvements being made in situations with new trains and where market growth is possible. Our analysis can therefore take on board the franchise savings promised by the bidders, although we must recognise the possibility that some may fail to deliver.

Note that reductions in subsidies required by franchisees include a number of cost increases. For instance, the net expenditure on insurance has risen substantially as the railway has been fragmented, with each train operator needing to be insured against all the others for £155m (aggregate) (or £60m for one occurrence). In the previous nationalised scenario, BR was only insured once. Similarly, safety validation costs are likely to rise – but these costs are already included in franchisees' subsidy bids.

However, franchisees have, as we have already seen, made assumptions about revenue growth which, in some cases, are substantial. Nearly all the franchisees have been more positive about the potential for revenue than were SDG in their pre-bidding analysis (SDG, 1993). If marketing and new trains really can bring in additional passengers and revenue, then this constitutes the type of private-sector market-driven approach which the Government was hoping for, not least because it reduces the call on the taxpayer.

With normal assumptions about discounting, we have taken the franchise bids and estimated the NPV of their savings relative to the 1995-6 out-turn position. We have extrapolated shorter franchises to 15 years at the level of the last year, but have also included a potential improvement in the SWT support payment, given our comments above that this particular franchise, as one of the first, was sold off relatively for proportionately more subsidy than would have been required later in the programme. We have assumed that the subsidy actually required for SWT for years 8-15 is £0. These assumptions show franchisees forecasting savings of around £2.5bn up until 2012.

One of the main benefits of privatisation is the easier access to capital for investment purposes. BR, as a nationalised industry, was undoubtedly hampered in some of its development projects by a sheer inability to raise finance, caused by PSBR pressures on Government expenditure, and the existence of the 'Ryrie' rules to prevent access to other private-sector funds. This impacts on the passenger through poorer-quality services. This is a cumulative effect; as each years passes, the backlog of investment is growing, and the impact on passengers grows likewise. Service interruptions caused by equipment failure, poorer ambience, and the inability to improve services (perhaps even if financially-worthwhile) are an outcome of this problem. As an order of magnitude, we have assumed that the current impact covers 5% of passengers, of whom 10% actually do not travel – this therefore gives 0.5% of current year revenue, which we forecast to grow by 10% p.a. The associated passenger disbenefits are necessarily larger than this; we have taken them as three times revenue losses, since this is a typical ratio.

Private-sector companies can be expected to make profits, on which tax revenues should be liable. We have assumed that 20% tax will be generated on profits of 10% of turnover, and in relation to current profitability; the ROSCO model is such that potential tax revenues are largest here, since these are currently the most profitable companies in the industry.

Adjustments to Ongoing Costs and Benefits

Logically, any analysis should compare what is forecast to happen under the new regime with that expected under the old. We have assumed that BR would have continued to reduce costs by 3% p.a. under OfQ, as it had for a number of years previously (and, incidentally, as LUL had also). Any privatisation must generate more than this, in order for it to be judged a commercial success. The NPV of these savings is around £1.5bn for BR (White, 1996b). Further, annual net savings of at least £70m.p.a. would have been expected from WCML modernisation.

In addition, an announcement by the Rail Regulator regarding a lowering of the track access charges was made before the franchise-letting process began. This means that some of the savings in franchise subsidy requirements are nothing to do with the increased efficiency of the franchisees, but would have occurred in any scenario with a Railtrack-type body. In fact, work by White (1996a) demonstrates that around 20% of the savings promised by franchisees are merely due to the reductions in track access charges payable to Railtrack, which makes some of the apparent franchise savings appear less impressive. We have, however, only used half of the reduction in track access charges in our calculations, as some of the previous efficiency gains were in infrastructure activities, and an adjustment for this has already been made in the preceding paragraph.

A third key adjustment is in respect of economic growth. Some of the franchise winners are clearly expecting economic growth to lead to increased travel and hence increased revenue. However, economic growth is largely independent of railway performance in an economy such as Britain's, and an improvement in the economic climate would therefore have occurred anyway. We have assumed that there is 1% economic growth for five years, followed by zero growth (assumptions which we feel are pessimistic), and that a 1% increase in GDP leads to a 1% increase in rail passenger revenue.

Lastly, an adjustment is required to reflect the fact that Railtrack's higher track access charges are not entirely due to the increased interface costs and its profit margins. When set up, provision was made for Railtrack to invest in asset replacement at a higher level than had been the case in recent years. This increase (from approx. £400m p.a. to £600m p.a.) was solely to reflect under-investment in previous years, and should be excluded from calculations. (In reality, however, as we have seen, Railtrack failed to invest at this level at first, but this shortfall should be addressed in the near future).

Note that it would be incorrect to adjust for the £500m debt write-off for Channel Tunnel freight traffic, since this would have been necessary in any event.

Results

Table 7.6 summarises our calculations for both the narrower (Government finance-based) and wider (Great Britain plc-based) analysis, with the latter (described as the net social impact) set out in bold. The results indicate that, whatever other benefits there may be from a privatisation process, the financial position to Government and country has deteriorated. Privatising BR in the manner chosen has probably cost the British Government over £5bn, and Great Britain plc considerably more. The magnitude of the costs derives largely from the number of interfaces which have been created within the new railway structure. However, it seems very improbable that, whatever the exploits of the new breed of operator, benefits will be found which exceed these costs.

As can be seen, the possible benefits of the medium- and longer-term in finding efficiency improvements are small when compared

Impacts of the New System – has it Worked?

		Notes
All figures are in £m, at an NPV of 8%		
Initial Costs and Benefits		
One-off (transitional) costs incurred by Government	-600	£50m + £12m per company + £15k per contract
incurred by others	-600	
Railtrack sale proceeds	1900	
ROSCO sale proceeds	1780	Hansard 15/11/96 p 637
Freight sale proceeds	325	
Miscellaneous sale proceeds	450	BRT, Res, IMCs, TRCs etc.
Railtrack & IMUs/TRCs: loss on sale	-2450	Some assets given zero book value, or sold too cheaply
Railtrack; public profits transferred	-69	
Debt write-offs	-1229	Hansard 15/11/96 p609
Track access grants to freight businesses	-575	Cost of 'packages' given to winning bidders for Freightliner and RfD
Transfer of liabilities to county councils	-1000	1000 bridges Hansard 15/11/96
Opportunity costs of delayed investment		Impact of hiatus in investment during privatisation process
Revenue	-425	
Benefits	-1275	
Temporary disruption to services	-3	Estimate of time lost through poor punctuality & cancellations
Ongoing Costs and Benefits		
Additional interface costs	-7104	£830m p.a. (from Hansard)
Benefits lost at interface	-1156	£135m p.a. (from SDG (1993))
Franchise savings relative to current position	6628	Including adjustment to SWT refranchise
Access charge adjustment	-1160	Only half of Regulator's requirement taken, as some previous efficiency gains were in infrastructure, and are included below
Regulatory costs	-171	ORR & OPRAF budgets
ROSCO tax revs (given £300m profit p.a.)	514	
Railtrack tax revenues (on £300m p.a.)	514	
EWS and miscellaneous tax revs (on £130m p.a.)	171	
Capital access revenue impacts	159	Impact of additional investment: say 10% of 5% of revenue, rising by 10% p.a.
Capital access benefit impacts	477	Three times revenue impacts
Jobs lost through temporary lack of orders	-27	Impact of hiatus in investment during privatisation process
Net Do-something financial position	-2343	Sum of above (excl. benefits figures)
Do-Nothing Position		
Expected efficiency savings 3% p.a.	4297	3% p.a. reduction in subsidy was occurring anyway, whilst WCML modernisation benefits were also expected
Expected economic savings	684	1% p.a. real growth for five years, then zero would generate more revenue
Asset replacement adjustment	-1712	Increases in asset replacement costs needed anyway
Net Financial Impact of Privatisation	**-5612**	**This is net cost to British Government**
Net Social Impact of Privatisation	*-9812*	*Figures in italics are net impacts to Great Britain plc*

Table 7.6 Analysis of the Net Effects of Privatising British Rail

to the initial increase in operating costs and the costs of privatisation per se. Furthermore, the additional costs imposed were very substantial compared to a lack of funds not only within the railway itself, but also elsewhere within the public sector, so the opportunity costs are considerable.

In summary, the key question about railway privatisation is whether efficiency and capital access benefits exceed set-up, transaction and regulatory costs, plus any other disbenefits, by a margin greater than would have been delivered anyway under OfQ. These results demonstrate that this is not the case; privatisation *in the form adopted* is very unlikely to have been worthwhile.

Company Impacts

Consideration of the impact of the privatisation process to the Government needs to be contrasted with the impacts on the companies involved in train operations and other functions in the industry. Importantly, profits will be made from train operations. We have already seen that Prism and GB Railways were set up specifically for the purpose of winning operating franchises, but there will be impacts on the longer-established companies too. Initial profit margins may have been lower than those elsewhere in the businesses of the more diversified companies winning franchises (see Table 6.5), but improvements are anticipated. For instance, Table 6.5 shows that GNER are currently making a profit margin of nearly 6%, but Figure 7.3 shows that they are looking to make perhaps 12% on their £250m East Coast business by 2002/3. Conversely, Prism's initial losses on LT&S look worrying unless they can be quickly turned around. The largest mountain to be climbed appears to have been taken on by Richard Branson's Virgin on the WCML franchise, however. A year-on-year increase of about 5% must be achieved if the subsidy payment reductions are to be met. Overall, with typical income growth assumptions being 3% p.a., it appears that any corporate impacts will be directly linked to the achievability (or otherwise) of forecast revenue performance. The jury is out.

Other Economic Impacts

There are a number of other economic impacts which should be mentioned, even if they cannot be evaluated. For instance, no new trains were ordered for 1064 days. This was undoubtedly the main reason for the closure of ABB's York Works, with the loss of around 1500 jobs. As the manufacturing capacity was lost to the economy (there being insufficient export orders to maintain the plant), and there is an estimated annual cost to the Exchequer of £9000 per person for each additional person made redundant (in terms of benefits being paid to them, rather than tax collected from them), we can estimate these other impacts. Together with a typical multiplier of two for employment in component supply industries, our assumptions suggest a further net cost of about £27m, even if employees found alternative jobs within a year. This highlights an additional and significant factor with the privatisation programme – the freezing of railway investment and development during the three-year hiatus period whilst the privatisation process was developed.

Once franchises were awarded, however, orders for new trains were indeed placed. The 1064-day hiatus was broken by a small order by Chiltern Trains for express units for their Marylebone-Birmingham services, but larger orders followed. Multiple-unit trains are being ordered to replace older locomotive-hauled services on both Gatwick Express and Virgin's Cross Country services. Virgin are also looking forward to replacing their HSTs in the medium-term. On the WCML, tilting trains may appear within the next five years as part of a step-change in services – but would this have happened anyway?

Other *employment impacts were* undoubtedly also considered when the initial decision was taken. Particularly with their historical perspective, Conservative Party leaders were aware of increasing public dissatisfaction with strikes in key industries, of which the railway was one. There were deemed to be industrial relations benefits if the railway was split up, since national stoppages would be less likely, as unions had to negotiate separately with up to 100 different companies. This was demonstrated during late Summer 1996, when there were indeed disputes with a number of the TOCs, but in some cases, passengers could make alternative arrangements more easily with other trains still running. That, of course, was a benefit for the passengers – and, hence, the economy, but not necessarily to all employees.

Railway wages continue to be low, and a unified national negotiating structure was one way in which workers in the rail industry might have hoped to see their incomes increase in real terms. However, a number of the newly-privatised TOCs soon led the way in removing some of the old working practices (including allowances for various elements of the job), and made train drivers and other staff salaried. Increases in basic pay were apparently paid for through increased flexibility, and reduced administration costs. Given these subsequent developments, there were probably benefits from privatisation – if only from the negative reason that the Government could no longer be called upon to interfere in what are now private-sector matters.

This chapter limits itself to first-order effects within the railway industry. It does not cover explicitly some macro-economic impacts such as on social security budgets caused by the more efficient use of labour in a privatised regime. As a consequence of privatisation, perhaps 10% of jobs within the railways may be expected to disappear completely (i.e. not to be replaced by jobs in sub-contractors), which implies a macro-economic cost of around £100m p.a. However, other macro-economic effects may provide a balance to such figures, which represent transfer payments only.

Environmental impacts would accrue if a change in railway structure led directly to changes in the traffic carried by the railway, especially if this traffic were diverted from other, more-polluting, modes. They might also occur if it could reasonably be shown that private-sector companies were less concerned with noise, smoke and effluent discharges. However, increasing attention to these issues across the country and in all sectors means that this has not happened. As there has been virtually no impact on traffic levels due to privatisation in the short-term, the environmental impacts are currently marginal, but these may become positive with the increased traffic promised by Virgin and EW&SR. EWS' continuing development of Transrail's Enterprise wagonload freight service to cover other parts of the country could be significant in transferring several percent of the lorries on Britain's roads back to the railways.

At a national level, privatisation of the railways may be seen as a missed opportunity in respect of 'levelling the playing-field' between road and rail modes. Rail privatisation arguably put the railways onto an economically-sound footing, but evidence continues to suggest that even larger subsidies continue to pour into the country's road network. Without road pricing, or other substantial economic changes in the transport sector, the overall economic position of the railways will remain broadly similar. Only Treasury-imposed reductions in the roads capital programme, an ongoing reduction in company car subsidies, and minor increases in the duty on petrol, are helping to redress the imbalance.

The *safety impacts* of privatisation have not been fully evaluated but, again, there appear to be different results in the short- and longer- terms. In the short term, the lack of orders for rolling-stock to replace ageing Mk I-type coaches in electric multiple units on the dc lines South of London certainly increased the risk of casualties in the event of an accident occurring. On the other hand, the inter-operator insurance-led worries have probably meant that those within the industry are even more aware of safety impacts than they were previously. Railtrack was widely criticised for delays in the EECSAP process of validating the operation of new rolling stock, but an underlying factor was the knowledge of the financial, as well as public relations, penalties associated with safety failures. (This begs the question, of course, as to the overall safety of the potential traveller priced off or otherwise discouraged from rail travel owing to safety concerns, who then travels by a more dangerous mode instead). It also assumes that the very real progress made by Railtrack in reducing accident levels amongst its workforce was not related to privatisation per se, but to other changes towards safer working practices, which appears to be a reasonable assumption. However, the net impact of a delay in introducing safer equipment tends to suggest that the impact of privatisation on railway safety was probably slightly negative.

Summary

The franchising process was a success relative to the previous restructuring of the industry. The variation in subsidy reduction

1957-built rolling stock still in use in 1997: DEMU 205001 at Oxted
[N G Harris]

largely reflected opportunities for market development, and the impact of new trains, with a base level of reduction of around 20% indicating the minor operational efficiency improvements planned, and track access charge reductions imposed by the Regulator. Later franchises required greater improvements in performance to be successful.

The overall scheme of railway privatisation has reduced employment in the industry, which may be seen as either negative (in terms of job losses) or positive (in terms of making the industry more efficient). Privatisation, whilst perhaps neutral in political terms, has not been a success in terms of either safety or, more significantly, financially. The process has cost the Government around £5bn. It can, however, reasonably be judged successful on the basis of improved customer satisfaction, and (to a lesser degree) on the impact on the environment following the greater levels of investment promised by companies able to borrow on the open market. If this investment does indeed increase the passenger demand levels by the amounts franchisees are planning for, that too has to be a success, but such improvements also occurred under corporate BR (e.g. following Transpennine service frequency improvements). Moreover, the latter did not put at risk journeys involving more than one train service, journeys which continue to be subject to problems.

However, any evaluation of privatisation is dominated by the financial impacts to the Exchequer and country, impacts which are very large and negative. They also conceal opportunity costs, in terms of other schemes on which the costs of privatisation might otherwise have been spent. Railway developments and refurbishments, or even expenditure on the National Health Service, prisons or schools, could have provided a better return for the country. Indeed, given the political difficulties associated with railway privatisation, the returns might also have been better on political grounds. If we were to award marks, an overall score of 4/10 for privatisation *in the manner selected* would be further reduced by the opportunity costs to around 3/10. The manner of privatisation was particularly weak, both in the number of companies created (i.e. the complexity of the resulting organisation) and in the hiatus which accompanied the development of the new industry structure. These problems look likely to exceed any possible benefits from the process. We must therefore conclude that Britain's railways have just emerged from an unsuccessful privatisation.

8 The Future of Britain's Railways

Introduction

Now that the new railway regime has been in operation for a year, it is apposite to consider the future of Britain's railways. This chapter looks forward to likely changes in the industry resulting from its complex organisational structure, and the way in which players within it are likely to respond to the incentives they have.

Operations

Some predictions for the new railway seem to be relatively safe. Administration costs will be cut. The total number of jobs will fall as the industry becomes more internally- efficient. Workers will have to become more flexible about hours; the re-introduction of 'lodging turns' (in which traincrew spend nights away from home) was already under negotiation as this was written, whilst advertisements for part-time staff were becoming more common, particularly for station duties. Investment will occur to gain efficiency e.g. Railtrack's programme of signalbox rationalisation in the South and West Yorkshire area, or EW&S's investment in new and more powerful locomotives to do the work of two old ones.

On the grounds of probability alone, the TOCs will have varying fortunes. It is believed that Roger Salmon, as Franchising Director, made an 'off-the-record' prediction that one of the 25 TOCs will produce political problems with super-profits, whilst another will fail. Prism Rail were, at the time of writing, apparently attempting to induce both of these simultaneously. Press stories highlighting the rise in their share price from 100p to 450p between March and December 1996, and the associated financial rewards to their directors, provide conflicting evidence to that shown in Table 6.5 in which they appeared to be making an operating loss. Meanwhile, other new TOCs were known to be having difficulties; for instance, train cancellation due to lack of drivers on South West Trains cannot have been forecast by their management.

Industry Structure

A rationalisation in the number of organisations is also likely, in order to capture some of the interface profits. Stagecoach now own both a ROSCO and TOCs, even if the regulatory authorities have commanded them to offer stock from the ROSCOs even-handedly to other TOCs. Consolidation has already occurred in the infrastructure maintenance area, with companies attempting to develop a nation-wide capability for track activities. Buy-outs of one franchisee by another seem probable, given bus industry experience, although OPRAF have made the development of monopolies difficult, by allocating franchises across so many groups. Smaller companies with only one franchise may, however, consider selling out to one of the larger players, or they may be taken over anyway.

Franchise winners may also wish to reduce their risks of geographical dependence. For instance, Connex's two franchises are both London suburban, and they are therefore particularly vulnerable to changes South of the Thames, whilst National Express are largely concentrated in the Midlands. We would expect a position to develop similar to that in the bus industry, with a small number of groups coming to dominate the market, by acquiring other companies where they can.

There is now a prospect of railway operators being profitable, albeit in the new and somewhat artificial market which has been set up. This would be a significant departure from historical experience. If the profits made by any one group appear excessive, the Regulator may be forced to intervene. Strong regulation will be needed in order to avoid the abuse of local monopoly power, and to avoid interface problems ruining the development of the industry. Regulation may also be needed in order to encourage investment, as has already occurred in the British water industry; the Regulator has already highlighted concern at Railtrack's under-investment in asset development (as opposed to maintenance), and further steps must be expected unless Railtrack reacts as required.

Some commentators have expressed surprise at the lack of *microfranchising* i.e. the sub-letting of operations within larger franchises. This could offer the possibility of the local development of rail services, especially for those services which are relatively self-contained. Whitehouse (1996) summarised the benefits as:
- labour flexibility offering cost savings
- local marketing increasing revenue

whilst disadvantages include
- central (e.g. adminstrative, safety registration, insurance) costs are higher due to considerations of pooling resources (Harris, 1988).

Stagecoach (with the Island Line) and Prism (with Cardiff Valleys) have both demonstrated that microfranchising is unlikely because the costs are more important. They have both saved costs by linking in franchise bids for these smaller units with other larger and nearby units (South West Trains, and South Wales & West respectively). Unless really small lines can re-register as a light railway, and save many of these costs, perhaps in conjunction using volunteers to operate steam services for the tourist market, we suspect that microfranchising is unlikely.

Wider rail markets are likely to grow, however, especially with ongoing environmental concerns. How much they do so is a function of their success in attracting new custom whilst coping with interface problems (e.g. connections and information) on the passenger side, and Railtrack's charges on the freight side. But it is in planning and developing the railway further that problems look more likely.

Planning

The complicated network of organisations set out in chapter 6 is going to have to work together if Britain's railways are not to stagnate, lose traffic and disappear completely. Continuing investment and development is essential. At all stages in the planning process (see Harris, 1992a, figure 1.1), input will be required from number of organisations, whilst others will have to give their blessing before new operations can begin. The complex nature of the new set-up is perhaps best understood by examining the manner in which typical planning processes will have to work in the future.

However, a few more general points can be made about investment. In theory, financing railway developments should not be too difficult, since passengers pay for tickets at the time of travel (or even before, in the case of season ticket holders). Cash flows are therefore promising. On the other hand, railways are capital intensive, with assets tied up for years. Companies might attempt to maximise profits by investing as little as possible; however, the Government have already indicated that they will be scrutinising tender documents to see what plans franchisees have for investment, as well as ensuring that assets are returned at the end of franchises in the state in which they were let. This means that franchises with new infrastructure (such as the East Coast Main Line) will tend to be more profitable, as cash is easily generated and investment needs limited. On the other hand, it will be a struggle for franchisees of older routes (such as the London – Southend line), since they will have to generate cash from revenues quickly and on an unattractive service, in order to finance much-needed capital investment. Indications that GNER's revenue for its first year is up around 9%, whilst LTS appears to be trading at a loss, may presage genuine evidence of this.

Investments involving more than one operator may become difficult to organise, especially if the returns are too small to excite the interest of particular participants (Harris, 1994). Mega-projects are going to have to require support from OPRAF, as provider of subsidies to the passenger TOCs, in order that Railtrack will be able to borrow to finance work. Railtrack (1995b) had already developed a number of options for the West Coast Main Line, but these took until the letting of the WCML franchise in early 1997 to progress significantly. A similar picture was true with the Thameslink 2000 project, which spent most of 1996 in limbo whilst other, easier, franchises were let. Eventually, that too was given the go-ahead when the Franchising Director gave his commitment to ensure the financial viability of the TOCs involved. This bears a similarity to historical precedent – as we have seen, Government intervention was necessary to support railway investment, as in the New Works programmes of the 1930s, whilst the private companies of the time actually managed to disinvest.

Rolling stock replacement

Replacing existing assets on a like-for-like basis is perhaps the minimum level of investment possible. Whilst operators of commercially-viable services will have a relatively free hand, they will require high rates of return in order to compensate them for the risk of new entrants to the market, for example. Unfortunately for them, the provision of railway rolling stock is not entirely straightforward; vehicles cannot be bought "off-the-shelf", and procurement probably takes a minimum of two years, with acceptance by Railtrack following that.

Operators of franchised services will also have to take into account the length of the franchise remaining. OPRAF have agreed to let franchises for longer periods if new rolling stock and other investment is to be forthcoming (e.g. for the Gatwick Express franchise). There is obviously a risk in buying new stock, even if some residual value can be attributed to the assets concerned (perhaps by selling the assets on to the next operators of the franchise). However, competition for leasing is expected, as manufacturers and other challenge the profit margins of the ROSCOs. Where stock can be acquired cheaply, one must expect operators to buy it, as with GNER's purchase of a redundant locomotive and sleeper stock for conversion into additional day-time seating capacity.

Electrification

This and other route development opportunities (e.g. new route alignments to increase speed) may be proposed by one or more private operators, who must persuade Railtrack that the improvements are generally worthwhile. Railtrack will then carry out such improvements, reclaiming its expenditure through enhanced track charges. However, an individual operator may find it difficult to get other operators to participate if they themselves are not ready to introduce electric trains, or if their operations do not pass under a significant proportion of overhead catenary. For instance, increased line speeds will be of little interest to operators of freight trains which may have a much lower maximum speed limit. Such complications associated with the development of the WCML have already become apparent. Railtrack may also have insufficient resources to carry out infrastructure improvements, which will tend to drive private operators to take over their own track (where they will have greater management control). More electrification is therefore perhaps doubtful.

Signalling

The interaction of track, electrification, signalling and rolling stock may cause significant problems; some operators may wish to introduce new signalling and control systems but find others unwilling or unable to cooperate. Again, the WCML modernisation programme gives examples and some sections of line may require several signalling systems (Railtrack, 1995b).

In general, railway development in the recent past has involved a complete package of measures (e.g. the recent Chiltern Line modernisation of the routes out of London's Marylebone station) where all issues are tackled together, since this is cost-effective and appears to bring benefits larger than the sum of all the parts. Moreover, some trains will only work with some signalling systems e.g. specific rolling stock is required for railways as diverse as London Underground's Central Line and the radio-signalled lines North of Inverness. Resignalling is therefore going to be a key area; skilled negotiators will be needed to ensure progress between Railtrack, authorities and operators.

The Construction of New Stations

Finance to construct new stations should be easier to arrive at, since the Treasury is no longer the only source of available funds. However, the costs of construction have escalated significantly with the introduction of Railtrack's profit margins, and interface costs. £500,000 for a small new station has become £1,000,000. Furthermore, operators must allow access to any such new stations to any other operator who wishes to use them (although charges may be levied). Interactions with other services on the line may be important; especially on the more heavily-used routes, trains which stop at new stations will tend to interfere with the running of those which do not. In addition, signalling modifications may be necessary to accommodate new stations, and these may be detrimental to the performance of trains not stopping, another issue which will require skilful negotiation.

The main change in this area looks likely to be a rise in the importance of property development companies. Stations such as at Ebbsfleet on Union Railways' proposed Channel Tunnel Rail Link will be financed by private companies whose returns will accrue more from development gain than from station operation. However, as planning authorities are likely to make the development gains conditional on station provision, there is a real incentive for the latter. In some cases, local authorities themselves may cooperate with property developers, for urban development and other planning objectives.

The Construction of New Lines

Development of Britain's railways might reasonably be expected to include a limited amount of new line construction to those places which have grown substantially in the 20th century and are without decent (if any) services now – New Towns such as Washington and Skelmersdale spring to mind. Private companies will be allowed to construct such links if they so wish, but a major drawback will be the EC's directive to allow other operators access. Railtrack could, of course, also construct such links if it were sure that its costs were likely to be reimbursed by future operations over the links concerned, and also if it had sufficient funding. So far, Railtrack has not yet looked to expand its network but is still attempting to maintain what it has. Joint ventures between the private sector and Railtrack may be a successful approach, although if the market is large enough (such as the cross-Channel market), private finance may be sufficient, as with the transfer of Union Railways to the private sector.

Major service changes

Over the last few years, British Rail's Regional Railways sector has introduced a number of completely new inter-urban services such as Liverpool–Manchester–Sheffield–Nottingham–Peterborough – Cambridge/Norwich, which have been facilitated by all the previous services being under one management. Similarly, in the London area, Thameslink services have been developed by linking together Network SouthEast services both North and South of the Thames, which had been under one management. In the future, there is a danger that such developments will be extremely difficult, and that the existing services patterns will become fossilised. It will be very complicated for OPRAF to develop new service patterns which do not transgress the problem of insufficient returns for the lowest participant (Harris, 1994), and the Thameslink 2000 project has highlighted some of the difficulties. Although some such services were developed when the railways were last in private hands, the power of the BR regional organisation in the post-war period stifled such initiatives because the services concerned would have cut across a number of different operators. Organisational matters alone may generate sufficient bureaucracy to prevent railway development, which would be a pity.

One key possibility, however, does appear to be the likelihood of developing cross-London international services. Virgin and National Express are both members of the L&C consortium building the Channel Tunnel Rail Link to St Pancras; both also have mainline franchises operating to the North. National Express already has services to Sheffield operating out of St Pancras, whilst a curve is to be built to allow access from the CTRL to the West Coast Main Line. This would enable Virgin's WCML trains to avoid Railtrack's Euston terminus in favour of its own St Pancras (thereby saving costs, as well as generating revenue by improving interchange for services to the Continent.)

Summary

The proposed railway framework is undoubtedly more complex than that it replaced. Those people who believe in railways as an efficient and environmentally-sound method of transport will have to hope that the finance, energy and ideas of the private sector companies proposing to run train services and stations can overcome the bureaucratic jungle that may overcome them if all does not go well. If the private sector cannot overcome these hurdles, inject investment and improve staff morale, the Government's wish to introduce private sector innovation onto Britain's railways will have failed and the entire country will be the loser. Railtrack's position and outlook will be critical for investment in, and development of, the industry. Whether in terms of rolling stock replacement, electrification, new line construction or major service changes, the omens are not particularly good, but the greater availability of private finance, in particular, may overcome these perceived disadvantages. Only time will tell.

9 Conclusions

The seeds of the privatisation of British Rail were sown in the industrial unrest of 1973-4. The defeat of Edward Heath meant that the post-War political consensus came to an end. Conviction politics became the norm and, on their return to power in 1979, the Conservatives set about putting their conviction policies into practice. Although the privatisation of the railways was discussed by many, it did not occur under Margaret Thatcher's premiership. It was left to John Major's Government to take the policy forward. Given the political climate of the time, and the ongoing poor financial performance of the railways, their privatisation in the 1990s was probably inevitable. The real questions are therefore, if privatisation was inevitable, was the method adopted the best one? How much has it cost us to get to the current situation? And what are the potential benefits?

Our brief historical perspective has demonstrated that few, if any, of the principles adopted more recently can be described as novel. The private development of railways in the last century, and their reorganisation and nationalisation in this century, have provided most of the ideas and evidence required for the current programme. Importantly, the current programme provided for both the restructuring of the railways, and their privatisation, as two separate steps.

We have examined the structure adopted, and found it very complicated. The sheer number of interfaces between companies clearly adds costs. The privatisation of this structure has had further impacts, as the profits earned within the money-go-round of the structure are no longer returned to Government, but to shareholders instead. We can be fairly sure that the method of privatisation adopted was not the optimum, whether examined in terms of Government finances alone, or Great Britain plc as a whole. Research carried out subsequently suggests that a split into around three passenger operating companies might have produced the optimum solution economically, implying that the 'Organising for Quality' programme had a lot to commend it.

Our analysis shows that the recent restructuring and privatisation programme for Britain's railways has cost at least £5bn net. This includes the forecast savings from the new franchisees, as well as the transaction, regulatory and set-up costs. It also compares the projected position from where the railways might have taken us, if OfQ had been left to develop. It is probable that, whatever the unquantified benefits of improved morale, or the potential for growth in the rail freight businesses, the privatisation has neither a financial nor an economic success. Attempting to take as objective a view as possible, we cannot see how environmental, political or other benefits might make up the shortfall. We therefore conclude that Britain has just emerged from an unsuccessful railway privatisation, which we would score 4/10 on its own. However, given the opportunity costs (i.e. what could have been achieved with the same resources), we award railway privatisation only 3/10. We hope to be proved wrong.

Whatever the costs already accrued, however, many of the disbenefits have now been incurred. We look forward to a regulatory regime which minimises the remaining problems (largely, those associated with the interfaces between different companies). We also look forward to the positive developments which should accompany the progress of the successful bidders, and to the investment the industry needs.

REFERENCES

Abbott, S & Whitehouse, A (1994) "The Line That Refused to Die", Leading Edge, Hawes (224pp., 2nd edn.)

Acworth, W M (1924) "The Elements of Railway Economics", 2nd edn., Clarendon Press, Oxford.

Aldcroft, D H (1968) "British Railways in Transition", Macmillan, London.

Allen, C J, Fiennes, G F, Ford, R, Haresnape, B A & Perren, B (1977) "The Deltics – A Symposium", Ian Allan, Shepperton (2nd edn.)

Andred & Ford, R (1993) "How Can BR Privatise its Passenger Fleet?", *Mod. Rlys.* 665-671.

Batchelor, C (1996) "All Change on the Railways", Financial Times, 29th October.

Box, D (1994) "The Relationship between Rail Operations and Track and its Effect on Charges for Infrastructure", *Transp. Econ.* 21 (3) pp 10-20.

British Railways Board (1978) "Railway Electrification", British Railways, London.

Burkhardt, E (1997) "Turning Round Freight", paper given to the Railway Studies Association, and reprinted in *Mod. Rlys.* 54 pp. 21-4.

Butterfield, P "Grouping Pooling and Competition", *Jnl. of Transport History*, vol. 7 no. 2.

Cochrane, R (1992) "The Management of Operations", ch. 10 pp. 105-116 in Harris, N G & Godward, E W (eds) "Planning Passenger Railways", TPC, Glossop (256pp).

Crompton, G (1995) "The Railway Companies and the Nationalisation Issue 1920-50", in Millward, R & Singleton, J "The Political Economy of Nationalisation in Britain 1920-1950", CUP, Cambridge.

Croome, D F & Jackson, A A (1993) "Rails Through the Clay. A History of London's Tube Railways", 2nd edn., Capital Transport, Harrow Weald.

Davies, J & Clark, R (1996) "Valley Lines: the People's Railway", Platform 5, Sheffield (96pp).

Department of Transport/British Railways Board (1981) "Review of Main Line Electrification: Final Report", HMSO, London.

Department of Transport, British Rail NSE, London Regional Transport and London Underground Ltd. (1989) "Central London Rail Study", HMSO, London.

Department of Transport (1992a) "New Opportunities for the Railways", Cmnd. 2012, HMSO, London.

Department of Transport (1992b) "The Franchising of Passenger Rail Services", October (168pp.)

Department of Transport (1994) "Britain's Railways: a New Era" (32pp).

Feinstein, C H (1965) "Domestic Capital Formation in the United Kingdom, 1920-1938".

Ford, R (1993a) "Implications for the Rail Equipment Sector", Transport Economists' Group Seminar on Rail Privatisation, *Transp. Econ.* 20 (2) pp. 37-41.

References

Ford, R (1993b) "Signalling Report is Railtrack's Poisoned Chalice", *Mod. Rlys.* 50 pp. 147-148.

Foster, C D (1992) "Privatisation, Public Ownership and the Regulation of Natural Monopoly", Blackwell, Oxford.

Foster, C (1994) "The Economics of Rail Privatisation", discussion paper 7, Centre for the Study of Regulated Industries (CRI) (32pp).

Fowkes, A S & Nash, C (1991) (eds) "Analysing Demand for Rail Travel", Avebury, Aldershot (192pp).

Glover, J (1985) "BR Diary 1978-1985", Ian Allan, Shepperton (128pp).

Glover, J (1996) "abc National Railways: a Guide to the Privatised Railway", Ian Allan, Shepperton (128pp).

Godward, E W (1987) "Return to Snow Hill", *Mod. Rlys.* 44 pp. 533-538.

Gourvish, T R (1986) "British Railways 1948-1973: a Business History", CUP, Cambridge.

Gwilliam, K M & Mackie, P J "Economic and Transport Policy", George Allen & Unwin Ltd., London

Hamer, M (1979) "Striking a Spark", Transport 2000, London.

Hamilton, K & Potter, S (1985) "Losing Track", Routledge & Kegan Paul, London.

Harman, R (1996) "The Railways Act 1993: New Opportunities on the Wrong Track?", pp. 65-74 in Terry, F (ed.) "Transport in Transition", CIPFA, London (160pp).

Harris, N G (1987) "To Privatise or not to Privatise?", *Mod. Rlys.* 44 pp 409-412.

Harris, N G (1988) "Economies of Massed Reserves for Transport Operators", *Trans. Econ.* 15 (3) pp. 25-31.

Harris, N G (1990) "British Rail Privatisation: a Few Myths Exploded", CIT Yearbook pp. 101-104.

Harris, N G (1992a) "Introduction", ch. 1 pp. 9-17 in Harris, N G & Godward, E W (eds) "Planning Passenger Railways", TPC, Glossop (256pp).

Harris, N G (1992b) "A Theoretical Basis for Apportioning Railway Costs", *Transp. Econ.* 19 (3) pp. 30-36.

Harris, N G (1992c) "Fares Policy and Logit Models", ch. 3 pp. 27-36 in Harris, N G & Godward, E W (eds) "Planning Passenger Railways", TPC, Glossop (256pp).

Harris, N G (1994) "Railway Investment and Privatisation", *Transp. Econ.* 21 (1) pp. 34-38.

Helm, J W E (1997) "The Grouping Years (1923-1938): a Comparative Study of the Railways in Crisis", Backtrack vol. 11 nos. 1, 2 and 3, Atlantic Transport Publishers, Penryn.

Henshaw, D (1991) "The Great Railway Conspiracy", Leading Edge, Hawes. (256pp).

HMSO (1995) "House of Commons, Transport Committee, session 1994-5 Fourth Report: 'Railway Finances' ", HMSO, London (two volumes).

Holley, M (1996) "Making Tracks: the Railtrack Story", supplement issued with Rail 284.

Jenkins, S (1995) "Accountable to None. The Tory Nationalisation of Britain", Hamish Hamilton, London.

Joseph, S (1989) "Rails for Sale?", Transport 2000.

The Labour Party (1932) "The National Planning of Transport", London.

Madgin, H (1995) "Modern Railways Privatisation Special", July (64pp).

Marsh, R (1978) "Off the Rails", Weidenfeld & Nicholson, London.

Mizutani, F (1994) "Japanese Urban Railways", Averbury, Aldershot (208pp).

Monopolies and Mergers Commission (1996) "National Express plc and Midland Main Line Limited: a report on the merger situation", HMSO, London.
Nash, C A & Preston, J (1996) "Railway Performance: how does Britain Compare?", pp. 99-106 in Terry. F (ed.) "Transport in Transition", CIPFA, London (160pp).
National Audit Office (1996) "The Award of the First Three Passenger Rail Franchises", report HC701, Stationery Office, London (74pp).
Nilsson, J-E (1992) Second-Best Problems in Railway Infrastructure Pricing and Investment", *Jnl. Trans. Econ. & Pol.* pp. 245-259.
OPRAF (1996) "Passenger Rail Industry Overview", OPRAF, London (242pp).
ORR (1994) "Competition for Railway Passenger Services: a Policy Statement" (36pp).
ORR (1995) "Railtrack's Access Charges for Franchised Passenger Services: the Future Level of Charges: a Policy Statement" (24pp).
Parker, P (1989) "For Starters: the Business of Life", Jonathan Cape Ltd., London.
Preston, J (1992) "Estimating the Demand for New Stations and Lines", ch. 7 pp. 71-86 in Harris, N G & Godward, E W (eds) "Planning Passenger Railways", TPC, Glossop (256pp).
Preston, J (1993) "Does Size Matter? A Case Study of Western European Railways".
Preston, J, Whelan, G, Nash, C A & Wardman, M (1996) "The Franchising of Passenger Rail Services in Britain", Institute of Transport Studies, Leeds.
Railtrack plc (1995a, 1997) Network Management Statements.
Railtrack (1995b) "A Railway for the Twenty First Century: the West Coast Main Line Modernisation Project", (56pp).
Railtrack (1996) "Annual Report and Accounts", Railtrack, London.
Railway Development Society (RDS) (1989) "Who Should Run Our Railways?".
Railway Development Society (1992) "A-Z of Rail Reopenings" (2nd edn.), RDS, Great Bookham, Surrey (86pp).
Railway Invigoration Society (1977) "Can Bus Replace Train?", RIS, London.
Ramesh, R (1996) "Private Railways face Hazards on Line", Sunday Times, 27th October.
Redwood, J (1988) "Signals from a Railway Conference", Centre for Policy Studies.
Ridley, T M (1992) "Getting Things Done", ch. 16 pp. 173-180 in Harris, N G & Godward, E W (eds) "Planning Passenger Railways", TPC, Glossop (256pp).
Salveson, P (1989) "British Rail: the Radical Alternative to Privatisation", CLES, Manchester (158pp).
SDG (1993) "The Costs of Rail Privatisation: an Initial Assessment".
Semmens, P (1991) "Electrifying the East Coast Route", Patrick Stephens Ltd., Yeovil (224pp).
Starkie, D (1993) "Competition: Myth or Reality", Transport Economists' Group Seminar on Rail Privatisation, *Transp. Econ.* 20 (2) pp. 26-30.
Stewart, V & Chadwick, V (1987) "Chaging Trains: Messages for Management from the ScotRail Challenge", David & Charles, Newton Abbot (190pp).
Terry, F (1996) "New Concepts in Financing Railway Infrastructure", pp 127-134 in Terry, F (ed.) "Transport in Transition", CIPFA, London (160pp).
Thomson, A W J & Hunter, L C (1973) "The Nationalised Transport Industries", Heinemann Educational Books, London.
Vickers, J & Yarrow, G (1993) "Privatization. An Economic Analysis", 5th edn., MIT Press, Cambridge, Massachusetts.
Warburg, S B C (1996) "Railtrack Share Offer Prospectus", London.

References

White, P R (1993) "Some Introductory Observations", Transport Economists' Group Seminar on Rail Privatisation, *Transp. Econ.* 20 (2) pp. 5-12.

White, P (1996a) "Estimates of the Financial Effects of Rail Privatisation", *Transp. Econ.* 23 (2) pp. 15-23.

White, P (1996b) private communication on the above, 3/12/96.

Whitehouse, M (1996) "Franchising the Regional Railway", TR&IN conference on "Re-inventing the Regional Railway", Manchester.

Williams, L H (1985) "APT – A Promise Unfulfilled", Ian Allan, Shepperton.

Wilson, D (1991) "Breakthrough: Tunnelling the Channel", Century, London (144pp).

Wolmar, C (1996) "The Great British Railway Disaster", Ian Allan, Shepperton (144pp).

Worthington, N J (1996) "Can Railways win More Freight? The Channel Tunnel and Doncaster's Railport", pp 83-90 in Terry, F (ed.) "Transport in Transition", CIPFA, London (160pp).

In addition, financial and other data has been taken from the Annual Reports and Accounts for British Railways Board (1973-95) and for FirstBus plc, GoAhead plc, 3i Group plc, John Laing plc, National Express plc, Prism plc, Railtrack plc, Sea Containers Ltd and Stagecoach plc.

Appendix A. Sales and Disposals of BR Subsidiary Businesses

Business	Purchaser	Date	Price £m
Transmark	Halcrow	7/4/93	6.7
Meldon Quarry Ltd	ECC Construction Materials Ltd	4/3/94	5.0
Special Trains Unit	Flying Scotsman Railways	31/3/95	1.3
Swindon Electronic Centre	ABB Customer Support Servs Ltd	13/4/95	0.4
Chart Leacon Level 5 Depot	ABB Customer Support Servs Ltd	5/6/95}	
Doncaster BRML Depot	ABB Customer Support Servs Ltd	5/6/95}	19.4
Ilford Level 5 Depot	ABB Customer Support Servs Ltd	5/6/95}	
Springburn BRML Depot	Railcare	6/6/95}	5.7
Wolverton BRML Depot	Railcare	6/6/95}	
Eastleigh BRML Depot	Wessex Traincare Ltd (MBO)	7/6/95	7.1
Baileyfield S&C Works	VAE-Baileyfield Ltd	7/7/95	1.3
DCU Birmingham	Owen Williams Ltd	25/7/95	1.0
IDG Glasgow	Scott Wilson Kirkpatrick	18/8/95}	0.6
Mainline Swindon	Scott Wilson Kirkpatrick	18/8/95}	
Ditton Timber Treatment Works	The Phoenix Timber Group plc	1/9/95	0.5
Red Star Parcels	MBO team	5/9/95	-0.3
Business Plant Engineering	James Scott Ltd (AMEC Group)	15/9/95	0.2
CEDG York	British Steel plc	15/9/95	2.9
OBS Services Ltd	MBO team	3/10/95	11.6
Quality & Safety Services/QAS	Ingleby (805) Ltd (MBO)	10/11/95	0.3
Rly Occupational Health Service	Occupational Health Care plc	30/11/95	0.7
Signalling Control UK Ltd	BTR plc (Westinghouse Sigs Ltd)	1/12/95	39.9
Rail Express Systems	North & South Railways Ltd	9/12/95	16.0
Powertrack Engineering Co	W S Atkins	15/12/95}	0.5
CEDAC Croydon	W S Atkins	15/12/95}	
BR Telecommunications plc	Racal Electronics plc	21/12/95	132.8
Interlogic Control Engineering	Adtranz Ltd	4/1/96	17.5
Scotland Track Renewals Co	Relay Fast (MEBO)	8/2/96	10.7
Scotland Infrastructure Maint Co	First Engineering (MEBO)	14/2/96	27.5
Loadhaul	North & South Railways Ltd	24/2/96}	
Transrail Freight	North & South Railways Ltd	24/2/96}	225.1
Mainline Freight	North & South Railways Ltd	24/2/96}	
Central Track Renewals Co	Tarmac Construction Ltd	29/2/96	2.9
Castleton Works	British Steel plc	14/3/96	0.2
Eastern Track Renewals Co	Fastline Track Renewals (MEBO)	15/3/96	11.0
The Engineering Link	MBO team	18/3/96	1.0
Interfleet Technology	MBO team	22/3/96	0.5
Western Infrastructure Maint Co	Amey Rlys Ltd (Amey/MBO)	25/3/96	15.0
College of Railway Technology	Advicepart Ltd (MBO)	29/3/96	0.6
Network Train Engineering Servs	W S Atkins	1/4/96	0.8
Eastern Infrastructure Maint Co	Balfour Beatty Ltd	2/4/96	29.7
Southern Track Renewals Co	Balfour Beatty Ltd	2/4/96	5.9
Sth East Infrastructure Maint Co	Balfour Beatty Ltd	2/4/96	14.4
Sth West Infrastructure Maint Co	AMEC plc	18/4/96	11.0
Central Infrastructure Maint Co	GT Railway Maintenance Ltd	19/4/96	18.8

Appendix

Northern Track Renewals Co	Fastline Group Ltd	24/5/96	4.6
Freightliner	MCB Ltd (MBO)	25/5/96	5.4
Nthn Infrastructure Maint Co	Jarvis plc	18/6/96	9.0
Western Track Renewals Co	Relayfast Ltd	23/6/96	8.5
BR Projects	MBO team	26/6/96	1.3
BR Scientifics	Atesta Group Ltd	18/12/96	
BR Research	AEA	20/12/96	
BR QAS Ltd	MBO team		
Railfreight Distribution	English Welsh & Scottish Rlys Ltd		100 (est)
BR Property Board			
BR International			
Business Systems	Sema Group plc		
National Rail Supplies Ltd (including Collectors' Corner)	MBO team/Unipart		
Nationwide Fire Services	SERCo Ltd		
Rail Operational Research Ltd	BR Projects Ltd		
Opal Engineering	W S Atkins		
Raildata/RDDS			
Railpart (UK) Ltd			
Railtest	SERCo Ltd		
Rail Direct (was TRMC)			
GRAND TOTAL			774.7
of which	Freight	346.6	
	BRIS	168.9	
	BRT	132.8	
	all others	126.4	

Government Sales

Porterbrook Leasing Co	MBO/Charterhouse	8/1/96	527
Angel Train Contracts	Prideaux/Babcock/Nomura	16/1/96	672.5
Eversholt Leasing	MBO/Candover	2/2/96	500*
Sparesco	Angel/Eversholt/Porterbrook	2/2/96	
Union Railways	London & Continental	1/6/96	
European Passenger Services	London & Continental	1/6/96	

Businesses Closed
Rail News
BR Savings Bank
Taunton Concrete Works
Engineering Development Unit
Grove Management Training Centre

Businesses Transferred to Joint Industry Ownership
First Procurement
Railpen Ltd
Rail Settlement Plan Ltd
Rail Staff Travel Ltd
Railway Trustees

Sources: Jane's World Railways, 1996-7; Local Transport Today 194; Modern Railways, Jan 1997 p.12.; BR Vendor Unit.

*plus an additional £80m dependent upon the acceptance and satisfactory performance of the Class 365 fleet.